Hungary

FODOR'S TRAVEL PUBLICATIONS

are compiled, researched, and edited by an international team of travel writers, field correspondents, and editors. The series, which now almost covers the globe, was founded by Eugene Fodor in 1936.

OFFICES
New York & London

Fodor's Hungary

Editor: Richard Moore
Area Editor: Victoria Clark
Contributors: Robert Brown, Eugene Fodor, Leslie Gardiner,
  George Maddocks, George Schöpflin
Drawings: Lorraine Calaora
Maps: Alex Murphy, Brian Stimson, Swanston Graphics
Cover Photograph: Stewart Cohen

Cover Design: Vignelli Associates

Fodor's

SECOND 2nd EDITION

Hungary

Reprinted from *Fodor's Eastern Europe*

FODOR'S TRAVEL PUBLICATIONS, INC.
New York & London

ISBN 0–679–01660–0

MANUFACTURED IN THE UNITED STATES OF AMERICA
10 9 8 7 6 5 4 3 2 1

CONTENTS

CONTENTS

FOREWORD

Travel to Eastern bloc countries has been definitely on the increase for several years now. Although all her neighbors have shared in the boom, it has been Hungary that has led the field and, as the most acceptable face of the Eastern Bloc to Western travelers, she now has a flourishing tourist trade going, developing every year. For Hungary is a country with a great deal to offer—fascinating art collections, historic cities, resort areas, sports, magnificent food and wine, and the chance to see an entirely different way of life. And all at prices that, if not bargain, are at least competitive with those in the West.

*

For the convenience of readers who wish to visit Eastern Europe, but want to limit their trip to Hungary, we have abstracted most of the material in this book from our current *Guide to Eastern Europe,* with added material. We hope that you will find it of help to you on your trip, and would greatly welcome any comments that you may have on your return home.

*

We would like to thank our founder, Hungarian-born Eugene Fodor, for writing an introduction to the country he loves so well; Lászlo Boros, Editor-in-Chief of Corvina, for his constant help and interest; and Gabor Tarr, Managing Director of Danube Travel in London, for his invaluable help and encouragement over the years.

*

While every care has been taken to assure the accuracy of the information in this guide, the passage of time will always bring change, and consequently the publisher cannot accept responsibility for errors that may occur.

All prices and opening times quoted in this guide are based on information available to us at press time. Hours and admission fees may change, however, and the prudent traveler will avoid inconvenience by calling ahead.

Fodor's wants to hear about your travel experiences, both pleasant and unpleasant. When a hotel or restaurant fails to live up to its billing, let us know and we will investigate the complaint and revise our entries where the facts warrant it.

Send your letters to the editors of Fodor's Travel Publications, 201 E. 50th Street, New York, NY 10022. European readers may prefer to write to Fodor's Travel Publications, 30–32 Bedford Square, London WC1B 3SG.

MAP
OF
HUNGARY

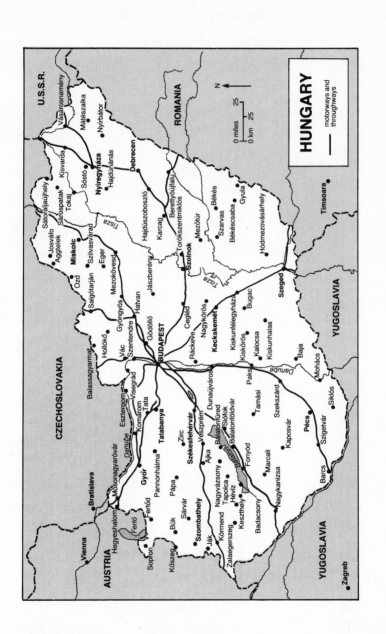

FACTS AT YOUR FINGERTIPS

FACTS AT YOUR FINGERTIPS

Planning Your Trip

NATIONAL TOURIST OFFICES. Most foreign travel to Hungary is handled via the offices of IBUSZ, the Hungarian national tourist office. It has many branches in Budapest, including desks in all the major hotels and in the more important towns. In Budapest, perhaps confusingly, different branches of IBUSZ deal with different aspects of travel; one with rail or air tickets, for example, another with hotel reservations and so on. However, the IBUSZ desk at your hotel will be able to help with problems of all kinds and will also exchange foreign currency.

Outside Hungary, too, IBUSZ offices can be very helpful. They can make your hotel reservations, obtain your visa, and book you on any of the numerous tours inside Hungary. They have numerous agents, such as, in the United States, American Express and Maupintour. IBUSZ offices will be able to give you a complete list of all agents accredited to them in your country.

In addition to IBUSZ, there are other official Hungarian agencies, such as Budapest Tourist, Volántourist, Cooptourist, Express, Pegazus and Lokomotiv, as well as a few semi-private agencies. There are also local tourist offices in all major centers.

The addresses of IBUSZ offices overseas are:

In the U.S.: 630 Fifth Ave., Suite 2455, New York, NY 10111 (tel. 212–582–7412).

In Canada: Hungarian Embassy, 7 Delaware Ave., Ottawa, Ontario K2P OZ2.

In the U.K.: Danube Travel Ltd., 6 Conduit St., London W1R 9TG (tel. 01–493–0263).

You can also obtain information from the offices of MALÉV, the Hungarian airline. Their offices in New York are at the same address as those of IBUSZ; in the U.K., their address is 10 Vigo St., London W1X 1AJ.

TOURS. IBUSZ offers a wide range of inclusive tours. Four tours covering different parts of the country—northwest Hungary, northern Hungary, southwest Hungary and the Great Plain—each lasting five days (four nights), cost around $180–210 a head for full board in a double room with bath. Also offered is a weekend in Budapest ($150–170) and a week-long visit to Lake Balaton ($230). In addition, there are numerous hobby tours, including accompanied bicycle tours, photo safaris, anglers' tours, visits to vineyards during the fall, cookery courses, weaving courses, keep-fit courses, agricultural courses and music courses; the choice seems endless. Tours for young people (under 30) are handled by the Express Youth and Students' Bureau.

To visit Hungary on a prepaid package tour is both less expensive and less troublesome than independent travel. A sample package tour, arranged by Danube Travel ex-London, to cover a seven-night stay in Budapest in a Moderate hotel with breakfast, return flight, a half-day sightsee-

1

ing tour and visa, but not transfer between the airport and your hotel, costs from £375 in the summer.

Riders will find that there are a large number of special riding holidays. Detailed information can be obtained from travel agencies abroad and from tourist offices in Hungary. There are holidays based on a stay at a stud farm and cross-country tours on horseback. A stay at a stud farm, which includes accommodations, all meals and tuition, ranges from about $40 to $70 a day, according to season and the comfort provided. Cross-country tours, lasting 10 days, with about 6 days' riding, cost from $700 upwards, fully inclusive.

From the U.S.: *Fugazy International Travel,* 770 U.S. Highway 1, North Brunswick, NJ 08902 (tel. 201–828–4488, toll free line 1–800–828–4488), offers perhaps the most comprehensive tours of Hungary outside of IBUSZ' own: four different 15-day summer itineraries cost $2,159 per person (including airfare).

Health and Pleasure Tours, 165 W. 46th St., New York, NY 10036 (tel. 212–586–1775), offer two- and three-week health spa tours of Budapest, with prices that range according to the package you choose.

From the U.K.: *Swan Hellenic Tours,* 77 New Oxford St., London WC1A 1PP (tel. 01–831 1616), run a 15-day "Art Treasures Tour" of Hungary in July and August. The tours are accompanied by a guide-lecturer; cost £1,325.

Wallace Arnold (Continental Dept.), Gelderd Rd., Leeds LS12 6DH, West Yorkshire (tel. 0532–636456), offers a multi-country coach tour that takes in Salzburg, Vienna, Budapest and Sopron, with France, Belgium and Germany en route—14 days, three of them in Hungary, from £439.

The Vienna office IBUSZ (Karntnerstrasse 26, tel. 51–55–50) organizes a whole series of tours to Budapest. A two-day tour, costing around U.S.$170 per person, covers bus travel to Budapest, lunch and a three-hour sightseeing tour, dinner with gypsy music, a night in a comfortable hotel, and a free morning for shopping, returning on the Danube by hydrofoil.

TRAVEL DOCUMENTS. Visas. In addition to a valid passport, all West Europeans (except Austrians, Finns and Swedes), Americans, Canadians and citizens of all Commonwealth countries require visas to enter Hungary. If you arrive by air or car, you can obtain visas at Ferihegy airport or on the border, otherwise you should apply to the Hungarian consulate in your own country or to an accredited travel agent before you leave. Even if you are flying or driving to Hungary it is advisable to get your visa in advance to avoid a tiresome wait as well as an additional charge. Send a valid passport and two passport-size photos to the Hungarian Consulate in New York, 8 E. 75th St., New York, NY 10021, or the Hungarian Embassy in Washington at 3910 Shoemaker St., NW, Washington DC 20008. In Canada, write to 7 Delaware Ave., Ottowa, Ontario K2P OZ2. In the U.K., write to the Hungarian Consulate, 35b Eaton Pl., London S.W.1. There is a fee of about $10 (£7 in the U.K.) and your passport must be valid for nine months after the date of entry. Visas are valid for a stay of 30 days.

Visas are no longer required for groups (with valid passports) staying for under 48 hours. This helps groups visiting from, say, Vienna.

Visas can be extended for a further 30 days by buying 300-Ft. worth of stamps from the post office and applying to your local police station. *All visitors must be registered with the police.* At hotels or private accommodations booked through an agency, this will be taken care of automatically. If you are staying with friends or relatives a 10-Ft. form must be obtained from the post office, signed by your host and taken, with your passport, to the local police station.

Passports. American Citizens. Major post offices and many county courthouses process passport applications, as do U.S. Passport Agency offices in various cities. Addresses and phone numbers are available under governmental listings in the white or blue pages of local telephone directories. Renewals can be handled by mail (form DSP-82) provided that your previous passport is not more than 12 years old. You will need 1) Proof of citizenship, such as a birth certificate; 2) two recent, identical photographs two inches square, in either black and white or color, on non-glossy paper; 3) $35 for the passport itself plus a $7 processing fee if you are applying in person (no processing fee when applying by mail) for those 18 years and older, or if you are under 18, $20 for the passport plus a $7 processing fee if you are applying in person (again, no extra fee when applying by mail). Adult passports are valid for 10 years, others for five years; 4) proof of identity such as a driver's license, previous passport, any governmental ID card, or a copy of an income tax return. When you receive your passport, write down its number, date and place of issue separately. The loss of a valid passport should be reported immediately to the local police and the U.S. Dept. of State, 1425 K. St., NW, Washington, DC 20524. If your passport is lost or stolen while abroad, report it immediately to the local authorities and apply for a replacement at the nearest U.S. Embassy or consular office.

Canadian Citizens. Canadian citizens apply in person to regional passport offices, post offices or by mail to Bureau of Passports, Complexe Guy Favreau, 200 Dorchester West, Montreal, Quebec H2Z 1X4 (514–283–2152). $25, two photographs, a guarantor and evidence of citizenship are required. Canadian passports are valid for five years and are non-renewable.

British Citizens. You should apply on forms obtainable from your travel agency or local main post office. The application should be sent to the Passport Office for your area (as indicated on the form). The regional passport offices are located in London, Liverpool, Peterborough, Belfast, Glasgow, and Newport (Gwent). The application must be countersigned by your bank manager, or a solicitor, barrister, doctor, clergyman or Justice of the Peace who knows you. Enclose two photos and a fee of £15.

Health Certificates. These are not required for visiting Hungary.

INSURANCE. The different varieties of travel insurance cover everything from health and accident costs to lost baggage and trip cancellation. Concerning medical treatment, there is no reciprocal agreement between Hungary and the U.S., so it is advisable to take out comprehensive medical insurance before you leave. British subjects are entitled, on showing their passports, to essential or emergency services including treatment in a hospital and the services of a medical practitioner; a nominal sum is allowed for prescriptions. But in any case comprehensive medical insurance is strongly recommended. Such medicines as painkillers can be bought at any chemist's without a prescription.

Travel insurance is available from numerous sources, however, and many travelers unwittingly end up with duplicate coverage. Before purchasing separate travel insurance of any kind, be sure to check your regular policies carefully. At the same time make sure you don't neglect some eventuality which could end up costing a small fortune.

Your travel agent is a good source of information on insurance. She or he should have an idea of the insurance demands of different destinations; moreover, several of the travel insurance companies retail exclusively through travel agents. The American Society of Travel Agents endorses the *Travel Guard* plan, issued by The Insurance Company of North America. Travel Guard offers an insurance package that includes coverage for sickness, injury or death, lost baggage, and interruption or cancellation of your trip. Lost baggage coverage will also cover unauthorized use of your credit cards, while trip cancellation or interruption coverage will reimburse you for additional costs incurred due to a sudden halt (or failed start) to your trip. The Travel Guard Gold program has three plans: advance purchase, for trips up to 30 days ($19); super advance purchase, for trips up to 45 days ($39); and comprehensive, for trips up to 180 days (8% of the cost of travel). Optional features with the Travel Guard Gold program include cancellation and supplemental CDW (collision damage waiver) coverage. For more information, talk to your travel agent, or Travel Guard, 1100 Center Point Dr., Stevens Point, WI 54481 (tel. 800–826–1300).

The *Travelers Companies* has a "Travel Insurance Pak," also sold through travel agents. It is broken down into three parts: Travel Accident Coverage (sickness, injury, or death), Baggage Loss, and Trip Cancellation. Any one of the three parts can be bought separately. Again, your travel agent should have full details, or you can get in touch with the Travelers Companies, Ticket and Travel, One Tower Square, Hartford, CT 06183 (tel. 800–243–3174).

If an accident occurs, paying for medical care may be a less urgent problem than finding it. Several companies offer emergency medical assistance along with insurance. *Access America* offers travel insurance and the assistance of a 24-hour hotline in Washington DC that can direct distressed travelers to a nearby source of aid. They maintain contact with a worldwide network of doctors, hospitals and pharmacies, offer medical evacuation services (a particular problem if you're hurt in an out-of-the-way spot), on-site cash provision services (if it's needed to pay for medical care), legal assistance, and help with lost documents and ticket replacement. Access America offers its services through travel agents and AAA. Costs range from $5–$10 a day. For more information, Access America, 600 Third Avenue, Box 807, New York, NY 10163 (tel. 800–851–2800).

Other organizations that offer similar assistance are:

Travel Assistance International, Europ Assistance Worldwide Services Inc., 1333 F St. N.W., Washington DC 20004 (tel. 800–821–2828), the American arm of Europ Assistance, offers comprehensive medical and personal emergency services.

Carefree Travel Insurance, c/o ARM Coverage, Inc., 9120 Mineola Blvd., Box 310, Mineola, NY 11510, underwritten by the Hartford Accident and Indemnity Co., offers a comprehensive benefits package that includes trip cancellation and interruption, medical, and accidental death/dismemberment coverage, as well as medical, legal and economic assistance. Trip cancellation and interruption insurance can be purchased separately. Call 800–654–2424 for additional information.

International SOS Assistance, Inc., Box 11568, Philadelphia, PA 19116 (tel. 800–523–8930).

IAMAT (International Association for Medical Assistance to Travelers), 736 Center St., Lewiston, NY 14092 (tel. 716–754–4883); 188 Nicklin Rd., Guelph, Ontario N1H 7L5 (tel. 519–836–0102).

In Britain, *Europ Assistance Ltd* is highly recommended and offers considerable help to its members. Multilingual personnel staff a 24-hour, 365-days-a-year telephone service, which brings the aid of a network of medical advisers to assist in any emergency. Special medical insurance is available for a moderate sum. Further information, plus details of their excellent insurance scheme for motorists, from 252 High St, Croydon, Surrey CR0 1NF (tel. 01–680–1234).

STUDENT AND YOUTH TRAVEL. From America. Students considering travel to Hungary might want to write to the Youth Express Travel Office there (Semmelweis ut #4, 1051 Budapest, Hungary). It has full information for student travel in Hungary.

HANDICAPPED TRAVEL. Facilities for the handicapped traveler in Hungary are limited. Those in wheelchairs in particular are liable to find few, if any, special facilities in hotels, places of interest or on public transport. Hungary has a Society for Rehabilitation at PO Box 1, H-1528, Budapest 123, and there is also a 12-page guide listing hotels in Hungary with facilities for the handicapped. But this is published in German only and is not available outside Hungary and Austria.

If you intend to visit Hungary, there are resources to help you plan. *Access to the World: A Travel Guide for the Handicapped* by Louise Weiss is an outstanding book, covering all aspects of travel for those with medical problems. Published by Henry Holt & Co. ($16.95), the book can be ordered from *Facts on File,* 460 Park Ave. South, New York, NY 10016. The *Travel Information Service* at Moss Rehabilitation Center, 12th St. and Tabor Rd., Philadelphia, PA 19141 (tel. 215–329–5715), can answer many inquiries concerning travel to specific countries and cities. So can the *Society for the Advancement of Travel for the Handicapped* (SATH), 26 Court St., Penthouse Suite, Brooklyn, NY 11242 (tel. 718–858–5483). Send a SASE for their list of tour operators who specialize in travel for the handicapped. One such is *Access Tours,* Ste. 1801, 123–33 83rd Ave., Kew Gardens, NY 11415 (tel. 800–533–5343; in NY 718–263–3835).

In Britain contact the *RADAR* (Royal Association for Disability and Rehabilitation), 25 Mortimer St., London W1N 8AB (tel. 01–637–5400). The *Air Transport Users' Committee,* 129 Kingsway, London WC2B 6NN, publish a very useful booklet for handicapped passengers entitled *Care in the Air,* available free of charge.

WHEN TO GO. From May to September is the best time, though July and August are usually hot and crowded. Spring and fall are often delightful and numerous fairs and festivals are held during the season. Winters are cold and the winter sports season lasts from late November through early March.

Average maximum daily temperatures in degrees Fahrenheit and Centigrade:

Budapest

	Jan.	Feb.	Mar.	Apr.	May	Jun.	Jul.	Aug.	Sep.	Oct.	Nov.	Dec.
F°	34	39	50	63	72	79	82	81	73	61	46	39
C°	1	4	10	17	22	26	28	27	23	16	8	4

SPECIAL EVENTS. The Budapest International Fairs take place in May (capital goods) and September (consumer goods). Other important events of international interest are the Formula One motor races and the Hungarian Grand prix, held early in August at the Hungaroring, just east of Budapest. Among the many art festivals are the Beethoven Memorial Concerts at Martonvásár, southwest of Budapest, in July and August; the Haydn and Mozart concerts in the Esterházy Palace at Fertőd, in western Hungary, in July and August; and the Open-Air Opera and Drama Festival at Szeged, which runs from mid-July to mid-August. The Budapest Muscial and Art Weeks are a traditional attraction of the early fall. Dates vary from year to year and details of these and other events can be obtained from IBUSZ or from its representatives abroad.

Among the many other special events are the following: **February,** Film Festival (Budapest). "Busó" masked procession on Carnival Sunday (14th) (Mohács). **March** (17–26), Spring Festival Week (Budapest); " Spring Days" (Szentendre, in the Danube Bend). **April** (4th), Liberation Day ceremonies (Budapest). **June,** Historical Pageant and Tournament (Visegrád). **June-July,** Folk-dance and Music Festival (Győr); Festival Weeks (Sopron). **July,** Summer Theater Festival (Pécs); International Equestrian Days (Hortobágy); Nyírbátor Musical Days—concerts in the historic church; "Agria" theatrical fair (Eger); Theater Festival (Szentendre). **July-August,** Helikon Chamber Music Festival in the Festetich Palace (Keszthely), Equestrian Tournaments (Nagyvázsony), "Szentendre Days of Music and Art" (Szentendre). **August,** Cultural Days (Hollókő); organ concerts in the Abbey (Tihany); Equestrian Show (Bábolna stud farm); Horse Show (Bugacpuszta); Equestrian Fair (Hortobágy); St. Stephen's and Consitution Day (20th), open-air performances, parade on the Danube, fireworks (Budapest); Baroque and Renaissance Concerts (Pécs). **September-October,** "Nyírség Autumn," cultural and gastronomic displays (Nyíregyháza). "Savaria" Festival of concerts and gastronomy (Szombathely), "Vintage Days" (Sopron).

Occasional concerts are given during the summer in the limestone caves at Aggtelek.

National Holidays. Jan. 1; Apr. 4 (Liberation Day); Easter Monday; May 1 (Labor Day); Aug. 20 (St. Stephen's and Constitution Day); Nov. 7 (Anniversary of Russian Revolution); Dec. 25 and 26.

MONEY. The unit of currency in Hungary is the Forint, which is divided into 100 fillérs (abbreviated Ft. and f.). There are coins of 10, 20 and 50 fillérs and of 1, 2, 5, 10 and 20 Ft., and notes (bills) of 10, 20, 50, 100,

500 and 1,000 Ft. The 10- and 20-Ft. notes are rarely met with. Note that there are two types of 10-Ft. coin, one large and silver-colored, the other smaller and yellowish.

The tourist exchange rate was about 47 Ft. to the U.S. dollar and about 85 Ft. to the pound sterling at the time of writing, but again this is almost certain to change during 1989. Traveler's checks are widely accepted, as are the usual credit cards—American Express, Diners Club, Eurocard, and Access—but these should not be relied upon in less expensive establishments or outside Budapest and the main tourist centers. Holders of Eurocheque cards can cash personal checks in all banks and in many hotels and stores.

You may bring in any amount of foreign currency, but you may only import—and take out—100 Ft. in Hungarian currency. Foreign currency may only be exchanged at official exchange agencies such as those in banks, travel agencies, hotels and airports. No foreign currency may be given or sold to individuals in Hungary. There is a black market in foreign currency in Hungary, but you will be tempting fate if you try to take advantage of it. Take care not to change too many dollars or pounds because although in theory 50% of money exchanged (up to $100 worth) can be changed back into Western currency, this may prove difficult in practice.

COSTS. At press time, mid-1988, prices in Hungary were still modest by Western standards. Even in Budapest and the larger tourist resorts prices are reasonable, while in the countryside almost everything can seem a bargain. But the situation is liable to change both before and during 1989. The introduction of up to 25% VAT on all service industries in January 1988 and the relaxation of price controls since April 1988 are guaranteed to result in price increases.

Sample Costs. Cinema ticket 20–60 Ft.; theater ticket 100–300 Ft.; concern and opera tickets cost from 100 to over 500 Ft. if someone famous is performing; beer from 40–60 Ft. in a bar, more in a restaurant; coffee (espresso) from 20–40 Ft.; scotch (glass) about 150 Ft. (but more in a nightclub or hotel bar); a bottle of wine in a modest restaurant 150–200 Ft.; a bottle of good wine in a first class restaurant 250 Ft. and up.

CUSTOMS. Objects for personal use may be imported freely. If you are over 16, you may also bring in 250 cigarettes or 50 cigars or 250 gms. of tobacco, plus 2 liters of wine and 1 liter of spirits, plus 250 gms. of perfume. In addition, small gifts not exceeding a value (in Hungary) of 1,000 Ft. each, to a total value of 5,000 Ft., may also be imported duty free. A 30% customs charge is levied on gifts intended for relatives and friends which are valued at over 10,000 Ft. in Hungary.

All personal belongings that have been imported may be freely taken out of the country. So may food for the journey, 2 liters of wine, 1 liter of spirits and 250 cigarettes. Gifts of a non-commercial character may also be freely exported, provided that they have been bought with hard currency or with forints obtained by the legal exchange of hard currency. Goods to any value bought from the Intertourist or Konsumtourist stores (for hard currency) may be exported without license, provided that the bill received at the store is produced at customs. You need a permit to export non-protected works of art valued at over 1,000 Ft.

For currency regulations see *Money*.

WHAT TO TAKE. The first principle is to travel light. Airline baggage restrictions vary, but most American and major European carriers allow two checked bags, one no larger than 62″ overall, the other no larger than 55″ overall (and neither more than 70 lbs.), and one piece of carry-on luggage, no more than 45″ overall. Several of the East European carriers, however, have stricter rules, limiting your baggage's *total* weight to 44 lbs. Check before you go. Penalties for excess baggage are very severe. But in any case, do not take more than you can carry yourself; it's a lifesaver in places where porters are scarce. In practice, this means more or less everywhere these days.

It's a good idea to pack the bulk of your things in one large bag and put everything you need for overnight, or for two or three nights, in another smaller one so that you don't have to pack and repack at every stop. Motorists should limit luggage to what can be locked into the trunk or boot of your car.

Clothing. Informal dress is quite acceptable for Hungary, though the smarter hotels and restaurants expect men to wear a tie for dinner. Pack lightweight clothes for summer visits, but take along a cardigan or sweater for cooler nights, also a raincoat. If traveling in winter you'll need thick woolens, heavy overcoats and boots or heavy shoes. Don't forget to leave some room in your suitcase for souvenirs and presents to bring back home.

Medicines and Toiletries. Take all the medicines, cosmetics and toiletries you think you'll need. Most items can be bought in Hungary, but some are difficult to find. If you wear glasses or contact lenses, take along the prescription.

LANGUAGE. Hungarian (Magyar) is one of the more exotic languages of Eastern Europe and at first sight looks forbidding. Generally, older people speak some German while more and more young people now speak English. Both languages are widely spoken and understood by those who come into regular contact with tourists. You will find a useful vocabulary at the end of this book.

TIME. Hungary is six hours ahead of Eastern Standard Time and one hour ahead of Greenwich Mean Time. From April to September (dates vary from year to year) the country operates on summer time, which is seven hours ahead of Eastern Standard Time and two hours ahead of Greenwich Mean Time.

Getting to Hungary

FROM NORTH AMERICA

BY AIR. As there are no direct services available from North America to Hungary, it may be easier to fly to Western Europe and pick up one of the numerous flights from there. Pan Am flies to Hungary twice weekly via Frankfurt, but this involves a change of plane from 747 to 737 at Frankfurt.

Fares. The best thing to do is to consult a travel agent, who should be able to arrange the best flight at the lowest cost. Sample round-trip fares as of end-1988 for travel NY–Budapest were: First Class $3,932; Business Class $2,156; Economy $1,038–1,105; Apex $789–841.

FROM THE U.K.

BY AIR. Britain is served fairly well for flights to Hungary. During the summer British Airways or the Hungarian national airline, MALÉV, operate at least one direct flight daily. British Airways use 737s on this 2½ hour run.

Fares. Standard fares are quite high, with the cheapest advanced purchase return—booked a month in advance and including a Saturday night in Hungary—at around £196, Economy Class at £408 and Business Class £502.

It might be worth considering an all-in package that includes the airfare. Using the Hungarian Tourist Office and staying in a 4-star hotel, a three-night stay in high season costs £320, with seven nights at £450. Out of season, three nights cost less than the standard airfare, and seven nights just slightly more. Contact the Hungarian Tourist Office for details.

BY TRAIN. The *Oostende-Wien Express* provides a useful all-year service from Ostend to Budapest. There is a connecting train leaving London (Victoria) at 09.00 for Dover and Ostend. In summer you can leave Victoria at 11.30 if you take the fast Jetfoil service. The train runs via Brussels and Cologne to Vienna (West) where it arrives at 09.04 in good time to change to the Wiener Walzer which leaves at 09.30 for Budapest, arriving there at 13.20 the same day. Light refreshments are available from Ostend to Frankfurt and a buffet car caters for breakfast from Passau onwards. Reservation on this train is obligatory.

Note: From January 1, 1989, the Hungarian State Railways joins the Eurailpass system—the 17th country to do so.

BY CAR. Hungary is better prepared for the foreign driver than many East European countries. There are more filling stations along the roads, BP and Shell are available, and gas can be bought for cash—Hungarian, of course, not for vouchers (except for diesel).

This does not mean that you should not prepare well for your trip. Get in touch with your motoring organization, and/or the National Tourist Office for full coverage of requirements. In the U.S., try the American Automobile Association, 8111 Gate House Road, Falls Church, VA 22042 (tel. 703–222–6811). In the U.K., both the AA, Fanum House, Basingstoke, Hants (or any of their regional offices) and the RAC, 49 Pall Mall, London SW1Y 5J9 (or any of their regional offices) can supply you with an International Driving License. There is a small fee.

Similarly, the Green Card, which gives full insurance coverage abroad, is not strictly necessary, but it would be foolish not to have one. They are also good for Western Europe, but are not required in Western Europe for citizens of EEC countries. They are readily available from insurance companies and cost from £5. In the case of a rented car, the rental agency will arrange it for you. Ensure that it is valid for the countries you wish to visit (and signed by yourself). For a rental car you will also need written confirmation of your permission to use the vehicle and a copy of the vehicle registration document. This last is also required if you take your own car.

Apart from your visa for Hungary, you should check on the requirements for any other Eastern bloc country that you may possibly pass through, or wish to visit, and their driving requirements. Some of them still employ a voucher system for gas.

The journey from London covers 1,100 miles and usually requires three overnight stops. The main crossing points into Hungary from Austria are at Hegyeshalom (Nickelsdorf) on route E5 from Vienna; Sopron (Klingenbach), southeast of Vienna and Koszeg (Rattersdorf) and useful for Lake Balaton area; Rabafuzes (Heiligenkreuz) on the main Linz–Lake Balaton route. All these customs points are open 24 hours a day.

Note that quite a number of frontier crossings between socialist countries are open only to nationals of these countries. Do not, therefore, be tempted by a less obvious crossing point without first making sure that you are entitled to use it, for you will only run the risk of being turned back. That said, it is worth avoiding major crossing points at the height of summer with their attendant queues. A slightly longer route is often rewarded by much lighter traffic and, sometimes, scenery that is less spoilt.

Good road atlases to buy are the *AA Road Book of Europe* and Hallwag's *Europa*. These are available from any large map bookshop, where you can also buy individual country maps. Specific information on road routes and conditions can be obtained from the Continental operations departments of your motoring organization.

Staying in Hungary

HOTELS. Accommodations should be applied for as far as possible in advance, especially in the less expensive establishments. Hungarian hotels are graded from 5-stars down to 1-star. These grades correspond closely to our grading system in the lists that follow of Deluxe (L) for 5-stars, Expensive (E) for 4-stars, Moderate (M) for 3- and the better 2-stars, and Inexpensive (I) for the cheaper 2-stars and 1-star. In practice the Hungarian grading system sometimes appears rather arbitrary, especially in more modest establishments, and to be decided by factors not always clear to the visitor.

5-star hotels have every comfort and luxury, including air-conditioning throughout. Only two 4-star hotels (the Béke and the Forum in Budapest) have complete air-conditioning, though many have this amenity in the public rooms; however, all 4-star hotels are extremely comfortable. 3- and 2-star establishments are less luxurious, though they are usually well furnished and well run. They are often crowded with package-tour groups, but this fact will rarely effect individual travelers. Single rooms with bath are scarce. 1-star hotels are generally simply furnished with few, if any, private baths; they are rarely recommended to foreign tourists, though in some provincial towns there may be no better accommodations available. The plumbing is satisfactory almost everywhere, though some remote (I) country hotels and tourist-hotels can be pretty primitive. Visitors from the West are made very welcome and service almost everywhere will be both friendly and smooth—though here, as elsewhere in Hungary, a tip can work wonders.

The table below shows approximate prices for rooms with bath and breakfast. *Balaton hotel rates include full board, which is compulsory at most hotels during the high season (June through August).* Hotel rates are considerably lower in many hotels in the low season; in Budapest, this is December through March (with the exception of the New Year holiday); in the Balaton area, where most hotels are only open from May to September, it is May and September.

During August two people in a double room with bath and Continental breakfast will pay approximately:

	Budapest	Balaton	Provinces
Deluxe (L)	U.S.$110–200	—	—
Expensive (E)	$100–145	$90–120	$60–80
Moderate (M)	$60–95	$60–80	$30–40
Inexpensive (I)	$15–55	$14–30	$10–20

For single rooms with bath count on from $20–35 and more per head per night. All singles in (L) and (E) hotels have private bath or shower.

In Budapest the (I) hotels which we have listed are generally comfortable and well-equipped; in the provinces they are sometimes less so, though they may be the only accommodations available in some of the smaller towns. There are no (L) and only a few (E) hotels outside Budapest, but the latest (M) hotels are usually very comfortable and well run.

In addition to ordinary hotels, there are also an increasing number of small guest-houses (often privately run), as well as many tourist hotels; these latter are for the less demanding and usually have at least five beds per room, with hot and cold running water in a communal bath- or shower-room on each floor.

Hungary has recently begun to turn some of its more picturesque and historic country houses into "country-house hotels." These vary in the comfort and facilities provided. Among them are those at Bük, Fertőd, Nagyvázsony, Szirák, and Pécs (Üszögpuszta).

Self-Catering. Bungalows with two rooms, fully equipped for cooking, etc., can be rented in Budapest and at a large number of resorts, particularly on the shores of Lake Balaton. Full details and rates can be obtained from tourist offices in Hungary and abroad, who can also arrange bookings. A typical bungalow for two at Lake Balaton costs around U.S. $300–450 a week.

Private Accommodations. Available almost everywhere, paying-guest accommodations are an inexpensive and excellent way of getting to know the people. In Budapest and in Lake Balaton resorts, the rate per night for a double room (single or double occupancy) is round $10–15, which includes the use of a bathroom, but not breakfast. A few rooms with private bath are available at higher rates. In provincial towns, the rates are lower. Such accommodations can be booked either through local tourist offices or by travel agents abroad. Applications should be made well in advance.

CAMPING. There are around 100 campsites in Hungary. They are to be found in all the country's chief beauty spots. Most of the sites cater to campers bringing in their own equipment, but a few provide tents. There are four categories of site, from 4-star to 1-star, depending on the amenities provided, and most are open from May through September. Caravans are permitted in all sites that have power points; a parking fee is charged for such caravans, as well as for cars, motorcycles and other forms of transport. At press-time, the rates for use of the site vary from approximately 80 to 210 Ft. a day, plus a charge for hot water and electricity. Young people between two and 14 years of age pay half these rates and there is no charge for children under the age of two. Members of the FICC are entitled to reductions of between 10–30%. *Camping is forbidden except in the appointed areas.*

Bookings can be made through the *Hungarian Camping and Caravanning Club,* Üllői Út 6, Budapest VIII, or through travel agencies.

Hungary has four nudist camps: at Délegyháza, some 30 km. (20 miles) south of Budapest; at Debrecen, in eastern Hungary; at Mohács, in the south of the country and at Balatonberény, on Lake Balaton.

RESTAURANTS. There are many excellent restaurants throughout the country, most, though not all, state-owned. In the large restaurants you will find an impressive bill-of-fare, often in several languages. If you want to eat really well, with famous Hungarian specialties such as goose liver, and with some excellent Hungarian wine, you should reckon on 600–1,000

Ft. a head at the very least in an Expensive (E) restaurant; you could pay more. In a good Moderate (M) restaurant, with half a bottle of wine, reckon on between 350 and 500 Ft. a head. On the other hand, for those with slender means (and not too large an appetite), there is often, even in quite high-class restaurants, an Inexpensive (I) fixed-price meal, called a *menü*, of two or three courses, which can cost as little as 60 Ft.; but in famous restaurants it can reach 100 Ft. or even more. This menü tends to be tucked away at the bottom of the bill-of-fare and to be in Hungarian, or Hungarian and German, only. Needless to say, the waiter will not usually draw your attention to it, but it is worthwhile looking for and often a very good value. Drink, of course, is extra. Most of the better places have music in the evening and prices are then correspondingly higher. Note that only the better restaurants and cafes have price lists in English, so make quite sure what you are ordering and, to avoid a possible unpleasant surprise, what it will cost.

There are also many inexpensive *önkiszolgáló étterem* (self-service restaurants), *bisztró* or *étel-bár* (snack bars) and *büfé* (buffets), which serve freshly-cooked meals.

Budapest is no longer a city of great coffee houses in the old Austro-Hungarian tradition, places where people met to discuss the topics of the day. In the capital, and indeed throughout Hungary, their place has been taken by a host of small *eszpresszó* (small cafes or coffee bars) and so-called *drink-bárs*. There are also numerous excellent *cukrászda* (pastry shops), where superb pastries are consumed, with or without the accompaniment of tea or coffee. For more details on Hungarian cuisine, see our chapter on *Food and Drink*.

It is usual throughout Hungary, in all the better cafes and restaurants, to leave your hat and coat in the cloakroom; the attendant will expect a tip of a few forints.

TIPPING. Hungarians have always been generous tippers and Communism hasn't affected this in the least. Although your hotel bill usually contains a service charge, tips are expected. You should be generous to the *főportás* (head-porter), who in practice supervises your stay. Then there is the chambermaid (who will get laundry done for you in a day), the breakfast waiter and the liftboy. Altogether, reckon to pay out around 15% of your bill.

In restaurants give the head waiter, who presents you with the bill, at least 10%; the money is divided among the staff. If a gypsy band plays for you and your table exclusively, you can slip a 100-Ft. note under the strings of the lead violinist's instrument or leave it in a plate provided for the purpose. It is up to you to welcome or reject his advances! Gas station attendants, taxi drivers and hairdressers all expect a few forints. In fact, if you are in any doubt—tip!

MAIL AND TELEPHONES. Postcards by surface mail to Western Europe (including, of course, the U.K.) cost 8 Ft., letters 10 Ft.; by air to the United States 10 Ft., to Western Europe 9 Ft. Letters by air cost 12Ft. to the United States, 12 Ft. to Western Europe. (There is little advantage in paying the airmail supplement to western Europe.) Stamps may be bought from tobacconists as well as post-offices. In Budapest, the main post office in Petőfi Sándor Utca, in the Inner City, is open till 8 P.M., Mondays through Fridays, and until 3 P.M. on Saturdays; closed on Sundays.

The post offices at the East and West stations are open day and night. Telegrams and telexes may be sent and long-distance calls made from the new post office at Petőfi Sándor Utca 17–19.

Telephoning in Hungary is usually easy; the system is automatic for almost all internal and international calls.

MUSEUMS. Hungary is rightly proud of its long and extremely rich cultural heritage, and has somewhere in the region of 500 museums and galleries scattered around the country, with a concentration in Budapest itself. Many of them employ very modern methods of display to show their treasures off to the best advantage, and mix both artistic and ethnographic items together to give a wide view of Hungary's past.

Some towns, obviously, are likely to provide museums of greater interest to the visitor that others. Pécs has several such—the Vasarely Museum, dedicated to works by the op-art artist, with 150 of his creations; a gallery housing sculptures by Amerigo Tot, the Hungarian artist who lives in Italy; ceramics at the Zsolnay factory; and another one-man museum, that devoted to the art of Tivadar Csontváry Kosztka. In Debrecen the Déri Museum was made possible by a huge gift from a silk manufacturer, and houses a wealth of lovely material from Chinese and Japanese art to Transylvanian embroidery. Szentendre, like Pécs, has several galleries, covering a wide variety of interests between them.

The larger and more significant museums open from around 10 in the morning to 6, some with seasonal adjustments. Nearly all are closed on Mondays, and on Saturdays admission is often free. Apart from Saturdays, there is usually a small entrance fee of a few forints.

The study and preservation of Hungary's past way of life is another area that has been devotedly followed over the past few years. Taking a leaf out of Sweden's book, Hungary has created several *skanzens,* called after the open-air museum near Stockholm. These bring together architecture and everyday objects from the past—bygones—in an imaginative whole. The largest is the Open-air Ethnographical Museum at Szentendre, located in a pretty valley near the town of the same name, just north of Budapest (25 km., 15.5 miles). There are other open-air museums, not so large but just as interesting, scattered around the country. A complete list is available from Tourinform. Because of the outdoor nature of these places they are mostly open in the summer months only, usually April or May to September or October. Like the other museums, they are closed on Mondays.

MUSIC AND FESTIVALS. As Hungarian is not the easiest language in the world to come to grips with, the many theater performances for which Hungary is justly famous are more or less a closed book to visitors—especially since they often involve sharply satirical material which would be over the heads of most foreigners, even in translation. But the fact that theater performances are not easily accessible to the non-Hungarian speaker is more than compensated for by the extremely high quality and wide variety of the musical offerings available.

Hungary is a country proud of its musical heritage—as any country would be that can boast Liszt, Bartók and Kodály among its great composers—and its rich musical life today measures up to the variety of its past. Visitors may be most conscious of the gypsy musicians who pop up all over the place, but the serious Hungarian will insist that these itinerant virtuosos do not really represent true Hungarian folk music, but only a schmaltzy version of it. It is rather with the many festivals, concert programs, opera performances and even up-to-the-minute pop groups that the real musical life of Hungary lies.

Budapest, of course, provides the focus for these events, with performances being staged all over the city and at most seasons of the year, locales ranging from the newly restored opera house to the courtyard of the Dominican monastery incorporated in the Hilton Hotel, from the open-air theater on Margaret Island to the courtyard of the Zichy Mansion, and in many other historic spots too. But Budapest is not the only city to have its musical life. Szeged has an open-air festival in the summer, so does Pécs. There are often Beethoven concerts in Martonvásár, another summer festival in Győr, the Savaria Festival Weeks in Szombathely, and orchestral concerts in the castle at Veszprém.

Some of these events are occasionally included in the tour programs of U.S. and U.K. companies, or you can find out about them from the National Tourist Office in New York and London (see *How to Go*). In Budapest there is a central theater ticket office at Népköztársaság útja 18, Budapest VI (tel. 120–000); tickets for the National Philharmonic Society's concerts can be booked at Vörösmarty tér 1, Budapest V (tel. 176–222), open from 11 to 6.

SPAS. Hungary is well known for its health spas. Nearly 1.5m cubic meters of curative waters gush daily from roughly 500 springs whose waters are good for bathing and for drinking cures. Budapest itself has a fair number, with 31 scattered throughout the capital.

Lake Balaton's north shore is home to Balatonfüred, one of Hungary's oldest and largest spas. At the southwest end of the lake lies Héviz spa, whose main attraction is the large natural thermal lake. Water temperatures are about 32–33°C, and never drop below 24°C regardless of the temperature of the air around it. The thermal spring feeding the lake is strong enough to keep all the water moving slowly clockwise. Overspill flows along a canal to Lake Balaton, and all the Héviz spa water is completely changed every two days. Other medicinal spas worth visiting are Balf, Bükfürdö, Gyula, Hajdúszoboszló, Harkány, Parád and Zalakaros. Most of the spas have comfortable hotels for those undergoing treatment.

An example of prices for a two-week treatment, from London, covering return flight, first-class accommodations in a double room with bath, medical examination and full medical care, full board with dietary meals where necessary, and spa treatment according to a doctor's prescription, varies from £780 to £920 in Budapest and £690 to £770 at Héviz. In all cases, accompanying adults without treatment pay less.

SHOPPING. Hungary is certainly not the place to be going in search of the international luxury goods that you can pick up in Western Europe. The things to look for here are handcrafted items—especially peasant embroideries and the exquisite Herend and Zsolnay porcelain. Hand-painted pottery and hand-made lace are also attractive, and there is some really excellent cut glass available. A very popular souvenir can be one of the dolls dressed in national costume, while records are usually of very good quality and fairly inexpensive. Hand-knotted rugs and attractive wood carvings are also available, while books on folklore and art are often produced in English and are amazingly good values for their high standard of illustration.

Frequently you will find an art or crafts shop with paintings, sculpture or limited-edition prints for sale, and these can be surprisingly cheap for anyone with foreign currency. There are several in Budapest, one of the best being in the National Gallery at the Castle, another in the bowels of the Hilton Hotel. (Note: there is a section on shopping in Budapest in the *Practical Information* for the Budapest chapter.)

There are three officially run chains of shops—*Utastourist,* which are located at the major frontier points such as Hegyeshalom and Letenye, and in Budapest's rail depots; *Konsumtourist,* which sell antiques, coins and other art objects; and *Intertourist,* whose shops are located in many of the main hotels, among other places. Usually these stores employ assistants who can speak English and other languages, and who are extremely helpful in coping with your shopping problems. All these shops sell for convertible—i.e. hard—currency, and you should keep your receipts in case you are asked to show them when leaving the country. Another name to look for is *Népmuvészeti* (Folk Art) stores, which, as the name implies, specialize in handcrafted items.

CLOSING TIMES. There is now a five-day working week in Hungary, from Monday through Friday, though most shops are also open on Saturday till around midday. The usual office hours are 8 to 5, banks 8 to 1; many shops do not open until 10 A.M. and close at 6 P.M.

ELECTRICITY. It is worth remembering that erratic plumbing and temperamental electric wiring have been traditional problems throughout Eastern Europe, and remain so despite much new building. There is little you will be able to do about it—you might find that even a change of hotel room only brings you a new set of little problems. Hungary is less bedevilled by these gremlins than some of its neighbors, but they are not unknown.

Hungary uses 220 volt alternating current. There may be slight variations in the current in local areas, but nothing significant. Sockets take 2-pin plugs throughout, so travel equipped with an adapter.

PHOTOGRAPHY. Snapping can be a touchy subject throughout Eastern Europe, but much less so in Hungary. There is an international sign that covers the situation—a camera in a red circle, crossed with a red line. It is mostly sited around army camps and the like, but you may notice it in and around airports. Photography from the air is likewise taboo.

Although you can buy film, it would be wiser to take a good supply with you.

NEWSPAPERS AND RADIO. Among the many foreign newspapers and magazines available in the leading hotels, you will find the *Daily News-Neueste Nachrichten,* a daily published in English and German, also such Communist papers as the *Morning Star.* During the main tourist season, there is a monthly publication in English and German called *Programs in Hungary,* which lists coming events.

Ten minutes of news in English, Russian, and German is broadcast each day by the Hungarian Radio, following the 12 o'clock news in Hungarian.

Sports

ANGLING. Angling is a popular pastime in Hungary, where fish from breeding farms are fed back into rivers and lakes at the rate of millions a year. Each species of fish has its own season, rigidly enforced, and the travel offices and local fishing clubs who issue licenses can tell you about the relevant dates. Visitors can get a fishing permit by showing their passports to the local water authority or the travel agency. General permits can be obtained from the *Hungarian Cooperative Enterprise for Game Trading,* MAVAD, Úri Útca 39, Budapest I; payment is by hard currency only. From May 1 to September 30, there is a fishing camp at Vonyarcvashegy, and another during August on Lake Valence.

HUNTING. With more than 700 hunting clubs and no entirely closed season, Hungary is increasingly popular with hunters of both small and big game. Much of the big game is hunted in the hilly and forested areas of Transdanubia, while the flat country is the place for small game. Deer are native to Hungary and wild boar can be hunted all year round. Mixed small game hunts are especially popular with visitors.

Accomodations for hunters range from a simple log cabin to a country mansion. MAVAD Hunting Office, 1014 Budapest Uri Út 39 and VADEX, 1253 Budapest, POB 40, will send you a price list and a contract specifying hunting conditions.

RIDING. Traditionally a nation of horsemen, there are now over 100 riding schools and stables throughout Hungary. These range from small holdings with two or three horses to large establishments with 50–60 horses and comfortable guest houses. Among the many options available are one-day outings, 10-day tours covering up to 250 km. (155 miles), and even courses in horse-driving. Hungary is especially well-suited to cross-country riders who have already acquired the basic skills. IBUSZ offices abroad will supply information and make reservations. In Budapest, TOURINFORM can answer any queries.

Dorthy S. Grant of *Holidays on Horseback,* 2420 44th St. NW, Washington, DC 20007 (tel. 202–338–2616), offers two-week tours of the Lake Balaton region for riders who want to spend four to six hours a day in the saddle with lots of galloping, plus other tours for those who prefer to take their riding more gently. Land cost from Budapest is $1,518, airfare additional.

GOLF. There is a golf course at the small village of Kisoroszi, about 38 km. (23 miles) from Budapest. At present the course has nine holes, but these will eventually be increased to 18. The clubhouse has a lounge, restaurant, and sports store.

SWIMMING AND BOATING. Lake Balaton and the Danube are the main centers. Yachts, rowboats, and windsurfers can be hired at lake resorts and sailing courses are organized for beginners. Sailing holidays on Lake Balaton can be arranged through IBUSZ SIOTOUR, Budapest V11, Wessenlényi Utca 26.

Budapest is dotted with swimming pools, many of them attached to the medicinal baths and mineral springs. Of the many pools, the largest and finest is the Palatinus Lido on Margaret Island.

WINTER SPORTS. There are few capitals in the world where you can take a bus-and-funicular ride or a 15-minute car trip to the nearest ski and toboganning slopes, but Budapest is one of them. The Buda hills cover an area of about 19 by 16 km. (12 by 10 miles); the skiing center is the Széchenyi hegy, but there are slopes for beginners and experts alike on the neighboring hills. There are other skiing centers in the mountains of northern Hungary.

Perhaps the most unusual winter sport is to be found on Lake Balaton, which generally freezes over to a depth of 8 to 12 inches. Here ice-sailing is a popular pastime from the end of December to the beginning of March and speeds of up to 96 kph (60 mph) have been reached. Even more popular is the ice-sled known as the *fakutya* (wooden dog).

Getting Around Hungary

BY TRAIN. There is an extensive network of railways. Standards are higher than average in Eastern Europe with buffet car expresses linking Budapest with a number of other cities. Country services are slow and less frequent. On the fastest express trains, seat reservation is obligatory. For those who like a lot of traveling, there are cheap Run Around tickets, allowing unlimited travel for 10, 20 or 30 days. Cost, 1st and 2nd class respectively, £80, £120, £161; £53, £81, £105. Details from Danube Travel, 6 Conduit St., London W1R TG. These fares are subject to change.

The Inter Rail Card entitles those under 26 to unlimited 2nd class travel for one calendar month in 19 European countries, including Hungary, and 50% of some cross-channel ferries and on Hoverspeed hovercraft services, plus 50% off travel in the country in which the pass is bought. Its current cost in the U.K. is around £140.

Also valid in Hungary is the Rail Europ Senior pass for those who already hold a local senior citizen's pass, entitling them to reductions from 30% to 50% on the railways of 17 European countries as well as a 30% reduction on Sealink cross-Channel ferries and Hoverspeed hovercraft. This card costs £5 in the U.K.

Note: Neither of the two passes described above is available to Americans, though American students who have been resident for 6 months in the U.K. are allowed to purchase the Inter Rail Card. As of 1989, however, the Eurail pass will be available to Americans wishing to travel to and around Hungary by train. The passes will be valid for first-class travel on express trains, have different durations (7, 15, 30 days or 1 or 2 months), and may be of different types (youth, couples, etc.).

BY AIR. There is no internal air service in Hungary.

BY BUS. An extensive network of medium- and long-distance buses operates throughout Hungary. But buses are always crowded and speed is not their greatest asset. Tickets and full information on the services can be obtained from IBUSZ or at the VOLÁN main long-distance bus station in Engels Tér in Budapest.

BY CAR. Hungarians drive on the right and the usual Continental rules of the road are observed. The speed limit for private cars in built-up areas is 60 kph (40 mph), on main roads 80 kph (50 mph) and on highways (motorways) it's 120 kph (75 mph); for cars towing trailers or caravans, the speed limit is around 20 kph (12 mph) less in each case. Seat belts are compulsory and drinking is absolutely prohibited; penalties for infringement are extremely severe. Any road accidents must be reported to the police within 24 hours. Visitors from the U.S. need an International Driving License; U.K. drivers are only required to hold a full British license. Detailed information on the documents you will need if you're taking your own car into the country is given on page 12.

Hungary's main roads radiate from Budapest. There are four *autopálya* (motorways), three of them only partly complete. The M1 now reaches

Győr on its way to the Austrian frontier (and Vienna); the M3 will, when it is finished, connect Budapest with Eastern Hungary. The M5 to south-east Hungary is now complete most of the way to Kecskemét, while the M7 leads to Lake Balaton.

In general the main roads, which have a single number, are excellent, as are many of the secondary roads. Many of the minor country roads, however, are either dusty or muddy, according to the season.

For roadside assistance, help with any legal problems after accidents or for tourist information, contact Magyar Autóklub (MAK), Rómer Flóris Utca 4/a, Budapest II (tel. 666–404); emergency service 260–668.

The Hungarian Automobile Club runs a 24-hour "Yellow Angels" breakdown service from Budapest X1V, Fráncia Út 38a (tel. 691–831 or 693–714). There are repair garages in all the major towns and emergency telephones on the main highways. Members of foreign automobile and touring clubs can pay any transport and repair costs by letter of credit.

Gasoline. Gas stations are marked on most touring maps of the country. A liter of gasoline (*benzin*) costs around 21 Ft. (a gallon is around $2). Unleaded gasoline, available at about 20 stations, including five in Budapest, costs around 24 Ft. per liter. Interag-Shell and Afor stations at busy traffic centers stay open all night. Otherwise stations are open from 6 A.M. - 8 P.M.

Car Hire. Several major car rental companies, including *Avis, Hertz* and *Europcar,* can make advanced bookings on rental cars in Hungary through the normal international reservations system. Fly-drive packages are also available ex-U.K. Within Hungary itself you can hire cars from major hotel reception desks or through the tourist offices.

Conversion Charts. One of the most confusing experiences for many motorists is their first encounter with the metric system. The following quick conversion tables may help to speed you on your way.

Motor Fuel. An Imperial gallon is approximately 4½ liters; a U.S. gallon about 3¾ liters.

Liters	Imp. gals.	U.S. gals.
1	0.22	0.26
5	1.10	1.32
10	2.20	2.64
20	4.40	5.28
40	8.80	10.56
100	22.01	26.42

Tire Pressure measured in kilograms per square centimeter instead of pounds per square inch; the ratio is approximately 14.2 pounds to 1 kilogram.

Lb per sq. in.	Kg per sq. cm.	Lb per sq. in.	Kg per sq. cm.
20	1.406	26	1.828
22	1.547	28	1.969
24	1.687	30	2.109

Kilometers into miles. This simple chart will help you to convert to both miles and kilometers. If you want to convert from miles into kilometers read from the center column to the right, if from kilometers into miles, from the center column to the left. Example: 5 miles = 8.046 kilometers, 5 kilometers = 3.106 miles.

Miles		Kilometers	Miles		Kilometers
0.621	1	1.609	37.282	60	96.560
1.242	2	3.218	43.496	70	112.265
1.864	3	4.828	49.710	80	128.747
2.485	4	6.347	55.924	90	144.840
3.106	5	8.046	62.138	100	160.934
3.728	6	9.656	124.276	200	321.868
4.349	7	11.265	186.414	300	482.803
4.971	8	12.874	248.552	400	643.737
5.592	9	14.484	310.690	500	804.672
6.213	10	16.093	372.828	600	965.606
12.427	20	32.186	434.967	700	1,126.540
18.641	30	48.280	497.106	800	1,287.475
24.855	40	64.373	559.243	900	1,448.409
31.069	50	80.467	621.381	1,000	1,609.344

BY BICYCLE. Cycling is not allowed on the single digit roads radiating out from Budapest—highways 2, 4, 5 and 6 and motorways M1, M3 and M7. Traffic on the two-digit roads is quite heavy during the week, while the three-digit roads pose few problems for the cyclist. Where you can, avoid roads indicated on tourist office maps by a thin brown line; these tend to be dirt roads. The yellow lines represent roads not recommended for racing tires. In Budapest itself you can cycle anywhere apart from the Chain Bridge and its approaches, the tunnel under Castle Hill and the expressway to Ferihegy Airport.

A day's cycling could take you to parts of the Balaton Hills; to the Valence Hills and around Lake Valence; to the Gödöllö Hills or the Bükk Mountains, to name but a few. As a general rule, you will find steep climbs in the Northern Range to the northeast of the Danube, with gentle hills to the west of the river. The east of Hungary, the Great Plain, is completely flat.

Costs for taking your bike by Hungarian Railways are 19.40 Ft. for up to 20 km. and, for journeys up to 100 km., 28.60 Ft. As express luggage the corresponding rates are 23.82 Ft. and 28.57 Ft.

Several cycling clubs operate in Budapest, including the *Central Sports Schools (KSI)*, 1146 Bp., Istvánmezei út 1; *Tipográfia Te*, 1085 Bp., Kölcsey u. 2; and *Csepel Sc*, 1212 Bp., Béke tér 1. Information on tour cycling is available by post from the *Hungarian Nature-lovers' Federation (MTSZ)*, 1065 Budapest, Bajcsy-Zs. út 31; tel. 351–930, 119–289 or 112–467. Mon.–Fri. 8–6.

Leaving Hungary

CUSTOMS ON RETURNING HOME. U.S. Residents may bring in $400 worth of foreign merchandise as gifts or for personal use without having to pay duty, provided they have been out of the country more than 48 hours and provided they have not claimed a similar exemption within the previous 30 days. Every member of a family is entitled to the same exemption, regardless of age, and the exemptions can be pooled. For the next $1,000 worth of goods, inspectors will assess a flat 10% duty based on the price actually paid, so it is a good idea to keep your receipts.

Included in the $400 allowance for travelers over the age of 21 are one liter of alcohol, 100 cigars (non-Cuban) and 200 cigarettes. Any amount in excess of those limits will be taxed at the port of entry, and may additionally be taxed in the traveler's home state. Only one bottle of perfume trademarked in the U.S. may be brought in. However, there is no duty on antiques or art over 100 years old—though you may be called upon to provide verification of the item's age. Write to U.S. Customs Service, Box 7407, Washington, DC 20044, for information regarding importation of automobiles and/or motorcycles. You may not bring home meats, fruits, plants, soil or other agricultural items.

Gifts valued at under $50 may be mailed to friends or relatives at home, but not more than one per day (of receipt) to any one addressee. These gifts must not include perfumes costing more than $5, tobacco or liquor.

If you are traveling with such foreign made articles as cameras, watches or binoculars that were purchased at home, it is best either to carry the receipt for them with you or to register them with U.S. Customs prior to departing. This will save much time (and potential aggravation) upon your return.

Canadian Residents may, after 7 days out of the country and upon written declaration, claim an exemption of $300 in Canadian funds a year plus an allowance of 40 ounces of liquor, 50 cigars, 200 cigarettes and 2 lb. of tobacco. Personal gifts should be mailed as "Unsolicited gifts, value under $40." For further details, ask for the Canadian Customs brochure, *I Declare.*

British Residents, except those under the age of 17 years, may import duty-free from *any* country the following: 200 cigarettes or 100 cigarillos or 50 cigars or 250 grams of tobacco; 1 liter of alcoholic drinks over 22% volume or 2 liters of alcoholic drinks not over 22% or fortified, sparkling or still wine, plus 2 liters of still table wine. Also 50 grams of perfume, ¼ liter of toilet water and £32 worth of other normally dutiable goods.

Returning from any EEC country, you may, instead of the above exemptions, bring in the following, provided they were *not* bought in a duty-free shop: 300 cigarettes or 150 cigarillos or 75 cigars or 400 grams of tobacco; 1½ liters of alcoholic drinks over 22% volume or 3 liters of alcoholic drinks not over 22% or fortified, sparkling or still wines, plus 5 liters of still table wine; 75 grams of perfume and ⅜ liter of toilet water and £250 worth of other normally dutiable goods.

THE HUNGARIAN
SCENE

INTRODUCING HUNGARY

by
EUGENE FODOR

Born in Leva, 100 miles north of Budapest, Eugene Fodor is one of Hungary's most noted sons in the West. His first Guidebook 1936 On the Continent *was followed in later years by a growing family of books that slowly gained a leading place on the travel scene, especially after World War II. His concept of an annually updated Guide was revolutionary at the time, though it was later imitated. The series spread its coverage steadily, until now, over fifty years after the first volume, Fodor's has a book on almost every country likely to be visited by the average tourist.*

Every world capital and major city has its promenade. Paris has the Champs Elysées, the pride of Rome is the Corso, New York and Broadway are almost synonymous, and Japan's Ginza is a kaleidoscope of color.

Budapest's version of the promenade is the beautiful Danube. The two halves of the capital are joined—even more than they are divided—by the wide, barely-tamed flow of these historic waters. On both banks the city turns all its alluring features toward the river, enhancing it with broad, patterned walkways and lush gardens. Hilly Buda and flat Pest cling to each other in a permanent embrace, joined by nine graceful bridges across the broad Danube.

On the one bank, Buda, the old capital of Hungary since the 11th century, is panoramic with old castles, steeples, ramparts and monuments—a fairytale collage of a romantic skyline. Pest, on the other bank, is modern, expansive, with broad avenues and fine turn-of-the-century buildings. It is one of the most spectacular cityscapes in Europe, a bustling, hyper-active business town, with a sprawling neo-Gothic parliament building, church spires, and art nouveau office and apartment buildings.

Grim reminders of recent history—the German occupation in World War II, the 1945 siege and the 1956 uprising—have almost completely disappeared, except for the ancient five-story-high synagogue. The immense castle complex of Buda and the charming streets of the historic hill capital have been completely restored; the downtown shopping districts on the Pest side are now pedestrian zones; deluxe hotels, congress halls and concert halls have been opened at the waterfront; and Budapest is again one of Europe's handsomest cities, a busy capital of two and a half million people. It nevertheless has the look and feel, when the sun is shining and the season is in full-swing, of an easy-going holiday resort, mainly due to the ubiquitous openair sidewalk terraces, garden restaurants, swimming pools, spas, and parks that cater to the outdoor life.

Exotic Variations

It all looks familiar, like one of Europe's most attractive major cities, yet the first-time visitor will also sense a faint feeling of strangeness about it all.

First, some of the language around you will have a totally alien ring to it. In Latin, Germanic or Slavic-language countries, the intonations often sound familiar. Not so in Hungary. Hungarian is an exotic element in the European linguistic babel. Central Asian in origin, its birthplace can only be guessed at, not pinpointed, as somewhere in the steppes of the Mongolian Turkistani highlands. It is said to be related to Finnish and Estonian, but these are philological speculations rather than proven similarities.

Similarly, food in Hungary is unique, with a pronounced, and delicious, flavor and texture. The same goes for the ubiquitous gypsy and folk music pouring out from every restaurant and coffee house. It lends a certain note of *joie de vivre,* and sets it apart from other Eastern Bloc countries where drabness of life is often the dominating mood.

However, Hungary is far from being an Asiatic country. Although it has been a Communist satellite for 40 years, in the wake of World War II which brought the might of the Soviet Union across the Carpathian safety belt and into the Danube basin, it is today among the most progressive of the Communist lands.

Yet, there are still some spots in the countryside where an exotic heritage reappears, mainly in the Puszta, purely Magyar with sprawling, squatting towns and villages amid the endless prairies stretching to the distant horizon. This is the land of the Csikós, horsemen who breed and control the sturdy Nonius horse and the gray longhorn cattle. The horsemanship of the Csikós is astonishing. I once saw a single horseman with a sheepdog regain control of a herd of panic-stricken horses running amok during a sudden violent summer storm. Such a feat normally requires a whole team of horsemen.

A different kind of landscape is to be found at Lake Balaton, Europe's largest warm-water inland sea with its Italianate western hinterland of Baroque towns and sunny vineyards on low hills.

Northeastern Hungary, Protestant and traditionalist, is the most history-minded part of the country and has many of the vestiges of the country's turbulent past. The fine wines of Tokaj and Eger have been produced on attractive hills here for centuries and its regional gastronomy excels in abundant game dishes.

Culture for All

Hungary is a big surprise and contradiction, an interesting place to visit if you want to see Communism in practice. It is even more interesting to watch it slowly lose its rigidity, consistently revising, modifying, experimenting with an immovable doctrine and procedure. Hungarians are past masters at such adaptability, successful and efficient ones, too. As a result—for the foreign visitors at least—Hungary is not only an interesting field for observation, but can also be an enjoyable country.

It offers outstanding entertainment, from high-caliber opera and symphony performances to the Budapest Spring Festival that blankets the entire country with 1,000 events in 10 days; from Formula 1 automobile racing, the only one in the East, to night clubs with topless floor shows on rotating dance floors; from a gambling casino in a 15th-century monastery tower to thermal spas and beauty farms; from elegant hotels to charming old inns, both with gastronomic feasts, fine wines and very stylish service. And always with music, music everywhere.

Cultural and sports events are usually subsidized by public funds and are low-priced. The government's cultural policy is to "broaden and expand culture horizontally" among the largest number of people rather than to deepen it vertically among an elite. As a result, opera, concert and theater tickets are very low-priced.

Artistically, such events provide a good chance to see creative talent often in confrontation with official policy. The Hungarian dramatic theater, for instance, is rich in new plays that cleverly express the nation's longing for more freedoms and often does so with such consummate skill and cunning that officialdom is simply unable to find grounds to prevent their production.

And all this is available at moderate cost. The deluxe hotels charge about one-half the Stateside rate while food, wines and entertainment are outright inexpensive.

The Spirit of Survival

Hungary is an intriguing country in many other ways, particularly in the character of its people. In spite of its martial reputation, Hungary has been victimized time and again by its unfortunate geopolitical situation. It was the venue for some of history's most devastating invasions, with successive waves of Tartar, Mongolian, and Ottoman imperial expansions from the East beginning in the early 12th century and lasting to the 17th. From the 18th century on, Hungarian history has been a saga of struggles against Austrian and German domination—wars of independence, revolutions against Austria in 1848, and finally defeat with help of the Russian czars. In modern times, Germany's *Drang nach Osten* led to World War I and to the dismemberment of Hungary.

Reduced to a small nation of 10 million, its landless peasantry emigrated to Canada, the United States and South America. Other waves of emigration followed: of the middle and upper class skilled workers and professionals, after the end of World War II, after the Soviet occupation and establishment of the Communist regime; and, again, after the 1956 uprising. Nowadays, this brain drain, this loss of human resource—of thousands of people dying, and hundreds of thousands fleeing the country—is recognized as a national disaster.

As a result, a Hungarian diaspora extends to all continents. Their extraordinary resilience helps to explain why the people of Hungary always emerged to achieve a certain prominence among small nations. They are now demonstrating a new vigor and, as always, an abundance and outpouring of humor. Within the Comecon marketplace Hungary is the chief supplier of jokes, particularly of the political variety. Humor is the nation's chief export. The offices, coffee houses, spas and other public meeting places produce a cutting wit of almost instant rapidity when, after, or before events occur. Whether the events are of world-shaking dimensions or just political scandals or sexual adventures, the Hungarian is usually ready, his mental rapier drawn to cut to the core the object of his dislike. Nothing is sacred or immune, and the target is often himself.

Living the Foie Gras Life

Another characteristic trait is the love of the good life. As highly qualified an observer as Nikita Khrushchev defined the Hungarian political system as "Goulash Communism." Today the Kremlin takes a certain pride in the Hungarian quality of life as if it were a product of socialist efficiency and productivity. The Eastern Bloc calls Budapest its "own Paris." This is where the ladies of the Kremlin send for their *haute couture,* where shops begin to repatriate a touch of elegance, where the tailor, the hat maker, the shoemaker and the dressmaker again start to prosper.

The country is fast becoming the role model for the socialist paradise. You could say that the current system is trying to evolve toward a *foie gras* socialism, the proverbial Hungarian penchant for the good life is no longer satisfied with the plebeian fare of goulash. It aims to consume all the *foie gras* the country so abundantly produces but still has to export to hard currency markets. Good food and excellent wines are indispensable necessities in the Hungarian definition of the good life, and fortunately there is an abundance of both for residents and visitors alike.

Since the almost total disappearance of the former middle and upper classes, a new generation of technocrats, bureaucrats, artists and, particularly, entrepreneurs are fast readjusting themselves to the prosperous western European middle and upper class styles and standards; they build villas in the Buda hills; here and there they buy a Mercedes Benz or a Peugeot; they dine out in town; they visit the West and travel overseas. And they are becoming more and more acclimatized to the ways of the West and know well how to enjoy them.

They like to see foreign visitors find pleasure in Hungary. There's no envy on their part, even if they cannot participate. Overseas visitors particularly are welcome. I often think the last area where Americans are genuinely popular is in Communist Europe, though this does not extend to the Soviet Union, where people have always feared contact with the foreigner.

Hungarians still cling to their traditions of chivalry and have preserved ancient notions of hospitality being a virtue and a duty. But beyond that, the appearance of foreign tourists coincides with the improvement of their own condition. And there is a feeling of cause and effect, that their own freedom to travel is at stake and that they are making significant progress when more foreigners visit their country.

The Welcoming Open Door

We must assume that any traveler to an Eastern Bloc country carries a fair amount of political curiosity in his intellectual travel bag. No visitor to a Communist land goes there in search of a suntan, a game of golf or a romantic encounter. Cultural, political, and social curiosity are more likely to motivate the choice of a destination. He wants to see how a different political system looks, functions, treats its own people, and plays host to its visitors. His curiosity is stronger than his apprehension over the possible "dangers" in visiting an Eastern Bloc nation. Hungary is one of the Iron Curtain countries where the tourist is safer than he would be at home. Public safety is maximal, accident rates are lower, terrorism is nil, the crime rate is minimal and tourists can circulate freely by car, train or any other conveyance—including horseback or bicycle.

Whether we like it or not, we have an adversarial political and ideological relationship with the Communist world. At the same time we are interdependent neighbors and fellow human beings inhabiting the same planet. A planet that is getting smaller every day, thanks primarily to travel and tourism. The only alternative to a nuclear "final solution" is coexistence, but coexistence can be hostile or pleasant. Hungary happens to be one country that, in spite of its different political regimen, exercises a genuinely open door policy toward its foreign guests and receives them with a smiling face. And we can reciprocate by accepting her invitation. We can discover a lot about the difficult art of survival there as well as about the art of enjoying life.

A COUNTRY AT THE
CROSSROADS

by
GEORGE SCHÖPFLIN

George Schöpflin is a specialist writer on East European affairs who teaches East European politics at the London School of Economics and the School of Slavonic and East European Studies. He visits the area regularly and has published widely on East European topics.

The foreign visitor arriving in Budapest will no doubt come with his or her particular baggage of preconceived ideas. What he or she will find at first glance is a city that is indisputably European and, at the same time, rather down-at-heel. It's almost like being in a time capsule and being whisked back to the '50s. The shop windows in the center, especially in the fashionable Váci utca, try to keep up with latest European fashions; away from there, in the districts where tourists do not visit, the displays are less elegant. The bustle and daily business of the capital give it an air of normality, quite unexpected in a communist country—a normality, that is, of the kind one would find in any Western city. The differences between Hungary and the West lie below the surface. They are real enough, but they demand more than a bit of digging.

Hungary was at the crossroads in the late '80s. In politics, in the economy, as well as in the way in which people lived, major choices had to be made. And a lot of evidence indicated that the choices had been left very late, with the result that they were more painful, more difficult than if they had been made earlier.

Much of the responsibility for this state of affairs rested with the person of János Kádár, Hungary's political boss from 1956 to 1988, and the system that he created. This system worked well for two decades, but as the men who ran it grew comfortable with it, they ignored the danger signs and, in this way, allowed the country to slide downward by the '80s.

Kádár's aims and ideas were fairly straightforward. He came to power in 1956 after the suppression of the Revolution in October that year. The Revolution had been a deep shock for the Hungarian communists, for they discovered that they had no popular support at all and the communist party itself vanished into thin air in a few days.

The new leadership, backed by the full military might of the Soviet Union, launched a new strategy. The population would be forced to accept the communist system whether it wanted it or not; but the system would, as far as possible, be made acceptable to them. In this way, Kádár and his lieutenants hoped that they would never again be faced with the collapse of October 1956.

The need to find acceptability led the Kádár leadership to look for economic solutions to a political problem. The Hungarian people might want a non-communist system, but that was not an available option. So, the alternative was a measure of prosperity, an opportunity for most people to better themselves. Consumer values—the acquisition of consumer durables, leisure time, trips abroad—came to replace the puritanical austerity of the Stalinist period.

But there was a price. Only the party, indeed only the leadership of the party, would have any say on what happened in politics. Political decision-making became the preserve of the few. On the other hand, the party would see to it that power was exercised cautiously. There would be a kind of self-denying ordinance to avoid the excesses that had made the Stalinist system so hated as to trigger off an explosion.

This particular system had its positive aspects in the short term and was reasonably successful for a while. But because it was based on a very conservative idea—do away with politics, allow only as much change as absolutely necessary—it was bound to come unstuck in the end.

The Economic Reform

The details of the story of Hungary under Kádár are relatively straightforward. Although he initially supported the Revolutionary government of Imre Nagy in 1956, he switched sides and agreed to head a pro-Soviet leadership to rule Hungary. The various social groups that were deeply committed to the ideals of the Revolution were suppressed in the late '50s, a process that ended with the successful conclusion of the collectivization of the land in 1961. This allowed Kádár to launch a policy of concessions and relaxation and, at the same time, to formulate a new strategy of growth. This latter became the New Economic Mechanism (NEM), the economic reforms of 1968.

The NEM has been the keystone of the Kádárist reform project. Ostensibly, it sought to make the economy more efficient by combining elements of planning and the free market. At the same time, it was accompanied by an improvement in consumption, both at the individual level and collectively by means of social welfare benefits. The idea underlying the NEM was that in every society there are conflicts of interest and this is something normal and natural— the wishes of employers and employees, producers and consumers, consumption and investment are not in harmony and, indeed, should not be.

By what criteria one is favored over the other, however, is a political matter, or involves politics beyond a certain point. And there was the rub with the Kádár system. Although at first there were vague promises that the NEM would be accompanied by an equivalent political reform in order to ensure that it worked properly, this never actually took place. There were too many well-entrenched, comfortable, vested interests that were decidedly hostile to making the NEM work properly. If it did work, then, for example, inefficient industries would suffer and those running them, work force as well as management, would lose out.

So there were plenty of people with a clear short-term interest in keeping the existing system in place and sabotaging the reform. They might not have been able to do more than slow things down, however, had the situation not been affected by outside events. When the NEM was launched, it was one of several major reform programs in the communist world. In the mid-'60s, the Soviet Union, the ultimate arbiter of what East European countries could or could not do, appeared to be looking favorably at economic reform. But then came the Czechoslovak experiment, the Prague Spring of 1968, which was eventually terminated by the Soviet-led invasion of August 1968. The implication was that all reform projects in Eastern Europe should be ended.

Anti-reform elements in Hungary interpreted this as the green light for a political counter-offensive. By 1972, they were successful. Although the NEM was never formally withdrawn, it ceased to operate in the way in which its designers had intended. Market elements were cut back and central control, partly through the plan and partly through a complex bureaucratic bargaining process that excluded market values, was reinforced.

It wasn't all negative. On the economic side, the consumer's lot improved a good deal. In the first place, after the terrible privations of the '50s, any consumer choice was welcome. The fact that there was enough food in the shops at affordable prices was a major improvement. As the '70s wore on, a growing number of people began to acquire a surplus income and they spent it on what their Western counterparts were buying—cars, dishwashers, weekend homes, or just conspicuous consumption.

The Impact of the Oil Shock

But by the later '70s, it became clear that disregarding the market exacted a price. The key event for Hungary, and not just for Hungary, was the 1973 oil shock. The Hungarian leadership decided that they would ride it out, that the crisis would be short-lived, and that they would take on Western credits to finance their policies. In economic terms, Hungarian industry was doing poorly, not so catastrophically badly as to prompt immediate reform, but the danger signs were there. They were ignored and instead central subsidies to unprofitable enterprises were kept up or increased.

But the leadership recognized that consumer satisfaction was essential for political stability. To ensure this, it permitted the emergence of what has come to be known as the secondary economy—in effect, space for individual and family enterprise, a chance to make a profit out of one's labor largely outside the state system. The peasant raising chickens on his private plot was an example, as was the town-dweller letting off a room in the summer to foreign tourists. This was a first-rate device and worked excellently until the mid-'80s, by when the accelerating economic deterioration forced many Hungarians to increase their labor in the secondary economy to near breaking point. There were people working 12–14 hour days, just to make ends meet. What had started as a way of tapping people's energies has degenerated into a system of self-exploitation.

Political Improvement in the '70s

Politically, too, the atmosphere was a lot better than in the '60s, let alone the '50s. People were free to speak their minds privately, they did not have to fear that if they grumbled they would be picked up by the secret police (as had been the case 20 years earlier). The intellectuals were given a deal, that in exchange for loyalty to the Kádár system, they would be relatively free to criticize the way in which it worked. This turned out to be a subtle device for ensuring loyalty. The fundamentals of the Kádár system were above criticism, of course, as was the link with the Soviet Union, but anything else was fair game. This set up an ambiguity about the limits of freedom, but at the same time, it created a broadly favorable climate of openness, which the intellectuals defended almost to the very end.

By the end of the '70s, the Hungarian economy was in serious trouble. It was faced with a balance of payments crisis, which was all the more serious seeing that well over two-fifths of the country's national income derived from foreign trade. The industries that were supposed to be the leading export earners, the sectors that did well out of the foreign credits, had no particular incentive to improve their productivity and output—why should they, given that their performance was assessed not by the market, but by the influence they had with the central authorities?

In effect, a lot of the money that should have gone toward building up modern, high-technology light industries actually went into propping up the declining steel, coal, and heavy engineering sectors, and into heavy construction and chemicals. In none of these areas was Hungary especially competitive. Indeed, by the early '80s, it was clear that Hungary, in common with the rest of Eastern Europe, had been overtaken by the economic miracle of the Far Eastern countries—a bitter pill, which Hungarian planners were most reluctant to swallow.

The country's situation was made worse by the Polish crisis of 1980–81, which prompted Western creditors to look at their East European loans harder than before, and by the Soviet invasion of Afghanistan, which led to a marked deterioration of the political climate. The Hungarians then embarked on a two-track strategy. They relaunched the reform and sought to persuade the West that Hungary remained a worthwhile investment. They proved to be rather more successful at the latter than at the former. The credits kept flowing as the '80s wore on, but too little of the restructuring that should have taken place—closing down inefficient enterprises and replacing them with competitive ones—was being put into effect.

Political Deterioration in the '80s

Very gradually, almost imperceptibly, the economic unease began to spread into politics. This took various forms. For a start, the party began to lose some of its previous confidence and, correspondingly, people began to lose their confidence in the party. Much of the responsibility—though far from all of it—rested with Kádár personally. It was his evident reluctance or inability to appreciate the need for far-reaching change that pervaded the system. There were various occasions when timely reform, involving a genuine commitment to opening up the economy and the political system, would have halted the slow downward slide and reversed the situation. Individuals and groups would have had their faith in the system restored and their energies and talents would have found adequate outlets.

By 1983, for example, there was growing pressure from the intellectual community on the party to embark on a "reform of the reform." This slogan was intended to summarize the various reform options—relaxation of the effective though informal control of the media, greater political openness to permit the unsupervised activity of interests and pressure groups, the democratization of parliamentary and local elections and the like. Kádár explicitly rejected any talk of "reform of the reform" and insisted instead on the "further improvement of the system." This was a euphemism for keeping things very much as they were, tinkering at the margins and hoping that somehow or other matters would improve. They did not.

Two outside factors impinged on Hungarian politics by the mid-'80s. The first of these was the alarming growth of Hungary's indebtedness to the West, going up steadily year by year, to reach around $16 billion by 1987, an enormous sum that even the most ardent defender of the Kádárist system found hard to explain away. The second was the Gorbachev succession in the Soviet Union and the pressure for reform from Moscow. The significance of this was greater than it first seemed. For years, the conservatives in Hungary were able to disarm their pro-reform opponents by arguing that, of course, they would love to adopt the kind of radical measures that were being proposed, but unfortunately the Kremlin would disapprove. With Gorbachev's adoption of *glasnost* and *perestroika* as the new Soviet agenda, this self-justifying argument lost all its force.

At the same time, the political constellation in Hungary began to change for the worse as well. Seeing that Kádár's system had the denial of politics as its centerpiece, it was actually rather difficult to have genuinely political—as distinct from economic—arguments heard. The way in which power was exercised was based on the complex interlocking bureaucracies that effectively excluded any overriding political decision, other than Kádár's own. Kádár, however, could not be everywhere and, in any case, he began to lose some of his energies as the years slipped by, hardly surprising since he was born in 1912 and was well past normal retirement age by the mid-1980s.

The outcome of this was the slow crumbling of the organization and discipline of the communist party. Communist parties are supposedly highly disciplined, dynamic bodies, the members of which accept instructions from above and ensure that the will of the party prevails throughout the political and economic system. This was manifestly no longer the case in Hungary by the '80s. What emerged instead was a kind of localization of power. Under this, local party bodies pursued their own policies often at variance, if need be, with the wishes of the center. So that if a particular enterprise, say, was run inefficiently and due to be closed down, the local party secretary would combine with other local notables to prevent this from happening. He and they all understood that, while the closure might have been useful for Hungary as a whole, their own local power would diminish. The overall result was a certain diffuseness in Hungarian politics. It became increasingly difficult to predict what decisions would be carried out and what would run into the bureaucratic sands. And all the while, the steady decline of the economy continued in the background.

To the Breaking Point

The breaking point, the moment when the Kádárist system crossed the irreversible threshold and lost the loyalty of some of its strongest supporters, came sometime towards the end of 1986. The clamor for reform came from several corners in the Hungarian intelligentsia. Above all, the reform economists whose advice had been repeatedly set aside in the earlier '80s, were able to express their views through an official body, the People's Patriotic Front (PPF). The PPF is a kind of umbrella organization that is supposedly there to act as the aegis for all social and economic organizations that are not parts of the party. Its leader at the time was Imre Pozsgay, an open-minded reformist who had been sidetracked into the PPF. Pozsgay brought the reform economists together to formulate a new, radical, economic reform project, which eventually emerged with the title "Turning Point and Reform."

This document served notice that the reform economists had lost patience with the hesitations of the Kádár leadership and were ready to express their disapproval in public. It was an important moment of change in a system that had consistently placed a high premium on attaching as much of the intellectual community to it as it could. But this was only the beginning of the breakdown of the cohesion of the intellectual community around Kádár. The party reformers were likewise impatient. They had been pressing, quietly at first, more loudly later, for the opening up of the system, for the party to pull back and allow the various conflicting interests that marked Hungarian life to come into the open. Increasingly, they were calling for pluralism and democratization. This last was intended to be understood as genuine democratization, in which parliament and the courts would play a real, as opposed to a pretend, role. Kádár ignored all this.

At around the same time, it became evident that the country's writers, always an influential group, were increasingly restive over a wide range of issues, such as the growing poverty, the decline of health standards, and the welfare of the large ethnic Hungarian minority in Romania, a painful and highly emotive issue. At the congress of the Writers' Union in late 1986, one of the conservatives from the leadership, János Berecz, in effect told the writers to stay out of politics, that their concern was superfluous and that the party knew everything anyway. This caused an uproar and many who had been loyal to the system now gave up on it. Much the same happened with the journalists, who had played a crucial role in keeping up the appearances of the system. Many of them had a very clear sense of the depth and extent of the crisis and were furious at being ignored. By the middle of 1987, all these influential groups had become favorably disposed towards the departure of Kádár and the launching of a much more radical reform program than before.

The final act before the toppling of Kádár in May 1988 took place in the party itself. The restiveness in the country, the sense of urgency that had come to affect the intellectuals, spilled over into the party membership. The leadership gave way sufficiently to call for a conference of party, to meet in May 1988. In the period before this gathering, and particularly during the delegate elections, the radicalism of the grass roots grew apace. The conference that convened in mid-May was not the obedient instrument that the leadership had come to know, but voted to eject the Kádárist leadership and to put Károly Grósz at the head of the party.

Grósz had been made prime minister by Kádár as a way of torpedoing his political ambitions to succeed him as party leader—a tactic that failed—and he was hardly a committed reformer. On the other hand, he had come to power with the support of genuine reformers like Pozsgay, so he had to make some concessions to them. During his first three months in power, these were mostly a matter of style rather than content, not the less important for that. The media were very open and previously taboo topics were freely aired; a whole range of informal activity that the party would have tried to suppress previously now flourished; and above all, the urgency of economic reform measures were daily being pressed on the public. Grósz played his cards close to his chest in his early days in power and made no immediate commitment to the radical reforms being demanded. The urgency of the economic situation was great, but timely measures could evidently halt the trend and initiate a slow, though painful, improvement. It was a major challenge.

Where things would go was very much an open question, though one of crucial importance to the people of Hungary. In the meantime, tensions were rising, though these were hardly likely to be too obvious to the Western visitor. All the same, in the late '80s it is hard to see Hungary as a prosperous and contented country— at times the stress, the atmosphere of tiredness and irritability on trams or in bus lines, is palpable. So the occasional moments of strangeness that one finds in another country—an unexpected or unpredictable response, say—can have many explanations. It may have to do with the distinctiveness of the local culture; or it may be the communist system that is responsible; but just as likely an explanation is the tension that Hungary and Hungarian society are currently experiencing.

A THOUSAND YEARS OF HISTORY

Hungary's Past and Present

A visit to Hungary will reward you with an experience unlike anything else in Europe. You'll feel the curious results of, on the one hand, being right in the center of the Continent, yet seeming to be curiously out of Europe, because of the language, the food, the music and the people—all different from anything you have seen and sensed elsewhere. The language bears no resemblance to those of its neighbors, for its nearest relatives are the tongues of the Finns and the Estonians, far away in Northern Europe.

Hungary—officially the Hungarian People's Republic—is a small, mostly flat country; to the west and north there are mountains, though few reach 3,000 ft. (914 m.); to the south and east stretches a great plain. Hungary covers an area of just over 93,000 sq. km. (35,000 sq. miles)—about the size of Ireland or Indiana—and has a population of about 10½ million. It is in many ways unique in Eastern Europe; it is more than the equal of its socialist neighbors in the warm welcome its kindly people give a foreign visitor; it has first-class hotels, an outstanding cuisine and excellent facilities for every kind of sport. Its capital, Budapest, with a superb situation astride the broad Danube, is not only a busy administrative and industrial city of over two million inhabitants, it is at the same time a great holiday resort and a famous spa. A splendid palace, an impressive Parliament building, great modern hotels and picturesque churches line the river; it is one of the grandest panoramic sweeps in Europe.

Then there's Lake Balaton, Europe's largest warmwater inland sea, with its charming, almost Italianate, landscape, its Baroque towns and its sunny vineyards on the hillsides. There's the Great Plain, a land of splendid horses and their riders, the *csikós,* and of fiery food and strong wine. Eger, in the north of the country, and Sopron, in the extreme west, are two of the loveliest Baroque towns in Europe.

Enormous strides have been made in recent years to improve tourist amenities and the best hotels—often built with Western help and knowhow—are probably the equals of those anywhere in the world. Only a few out-of-the-way provincial places still have older establishments with lower standards. Food is excellent almost everywhere, though one may still occasionally come across slow and off-hand service. But things get better year by year and a visit to Hungary is now very far from being the "adventure" it was only a few years ago.

Before St. Stephen

First in recorded history came the Romans, who built forts and camps for their legions, amphitheaters for their games, and aqueducts for their sumptuous baths. They called Western Hungary Pannonia—but they withdrew from Pannonia when the barbarians besieged their declining empire. Next came Attila, the Scourge of God, with his Huns. (It was at one time thought that the Hungarians derived their Western name from these wiry horsemen; this view is no longer held and the Hungarian Academy derives the word 'Hungar' from an ancient Turkic word "on-ogur," meaning "ten tribes." This dates from the 5th century AD, at a time when the nomadic tribes, which later became the Hungarian and Turkish races, were in close contact in what is now Southern Russia. Their own name has been Magyars, members of the Finno-Ugric division of the Ural-Altaic peoples.) After the Huns came the Avars, of whom little is known. They were vanquished in their turn by Charlemagne.

The Magyars originated from the region of the Ural mountains. They came to present-day Hungary in the 9th century—the generally agreed date of the "taking of the land" is AD 896. By that time—apart from a few Avar settlements—Svatopluk, King of Moravia, ruled Western Hungary. The picturesque folktales tell the manner in which Árpád, the first chieftain or prince of Hungary, proclaimed his intention of conquering the country. He had been chosen leader by seven tribes; according to the ancient custom they raised him on his shields; then the seven chiefs of the seven tribes each opened a vein in their arms and let their blood spurt into a common vessel to seal their blood-pact.

So the united nation of Magyars was born. When Árpád reached the Verecke pass over the Carpathians, he sent a beautiful white stallion to King Svatopluk, asking him only for some earth, water and grass in return. He saw that the earth was rich, black soil, easy to till; that the water was clear and fresh; that the grass was abundant.

Árpád promptly declared that by giving him these gifts, Svatopluk had ceded the country to the Hungarians; and when the Moravian king protested against such a sweeping interpretation of his intentions, the swift horsemen of the Hungarians routed his army. Within a comparatively short time the Carpathian mountains embraced a country ruled by the Magyars. Their mounted forays ranged deep into Europe, into Germany, France, Switzerland, Italy; the Western princes used them often as allies in their dynastic and internecine warfare. But finally they were beaten and retreated within their frontiers. This, and the fact that in the 11th century they embraced Christianity, saved them from the fate of the Avars.

The Holy Crown

St. Stephen, the first king of Hungary (1000–1038), was born a pagan, but he founded monasteries, built churches and brought Western craftsmen and artisans to his nascent country, and married Gisela, a Bavarian princess. Above all, he created a strong centralized monarchy, crushing a number of bloody revolts. Pope Sylvester II sent him a crown, and he was anointed king of Hungary in a solemn ceremony. He used foreign ideas and institutions but adapted them to suit the Magyars.

Though St. Stephen had no direct heir (his only son, St. Imre or Emery, died young), the Árpád Dynasty endured for three centuries. It was St. Stephen who broke consciously and definitely with the heritage of the East and, for better or worse, linked his country's fate to the West. He also severed all connection with Eastern Christianity, the influence of Byzantium, choosing the Church of Rome.

In the subsequent centuries, Hungary developed as a feudal country on the model of the other monarchies of Europe, with magnates, a landed gentry and a large mass of serfs. Its Magna Carta was called the Golden Bull, issued only 7 years after the signing of the Magna Carta at Runnymede. In the 11th and 12th centuries, the Magyars had to fight many battles to preserve their independence against successive German attacks. The 13th century brought a Mongol invasion that laid the whole land waste. The nation managed to survive, but the monarchy itself was weakened under St. Stephen's successors, and the Magyar equivalents of the English barons and the French *seigneurs* flourished in growing anarchy.

With the extinction of the Árpád Dynasty in 1301 came two kings of the Anjou (Angevin) Dynasty. Charles Robert reestablished royal authority and curbed the robber barons. His son, Louis the Great, extended Hungary's frontiers to the Baltic and the Adriatic and was the "paramount knight" of his age. Princes and savants flocked to his court and bitter international disputes were submitted to his judgment.

The growing power of the Turks with the expansive aims of the Ottoman Empire began to menace Hungary in the 15th century. Sigismund—later Holy Roman Emperor—was crowned king of Hungary in 1387, having eliminated various rival factions. He was far more interested in his German and Czech possessions than in Hungary; his chronic financial difficulties made him pawn 13 Hungarian mining and manufacturing towns in the north. His vacillating reign fatally weakened Hungary. János Hunyadi, who came from Wallachia, attached himself to Hungary and became its most brilliant general. But he tried in vain to stem the Turkish tide, though he had some temporary successes and the noontime ringing of bells in Christendom still commemorates his great victory at Belgrade. Hunyadi was also the father of Hungary's brilliant Renaissance king, Matthias (Matthias Corvinus, 1458–90), the last truly national monarch, who was elected by mass acclaim on the frozen Danube.

Matthias and the Turks

Nicknamed "Matthias the Just," he restored and enlarged the great castle of Visegrád; his Italian architect is said to have built 350 rooms, which were filled with glittering treasures. Here he held his dazzling court, and from here he started on his elaborate hunting expeditions. After his death, "King Matthias is dead, justice is gone!" was a popular saying. His famous library, whose beautifully-bound volumes were called Corvinas (his heraldic emblem was the raven, *corvus* in Latin), was scattered all over Europe, though a few dozen are still preserved in Budapest. Matthias built up the economic strength and created a short-lived, but nonetheless brilliant, Renaissance court. His army, the "black host," was one of perfectly-trained mercenaries. He was the wielder of considerable power in Central and Western Europe during the 32 years of his reign. But he left only a weak, illegitimate heir, and the series of ineffectual kings (of Czech and Polish origin) who followed gave a free hand to feudal development.

In 1514, when a crusade was proclaimed against the Turks, the peasants rose against the unbearable burden of taxation and corvée. Led by George Dózsa, a member of the minor gentry, they fought the nobles, but lost in the end to superior armament and strategic skill. Dózsa was roasted alive on an iron throne and his followers were forced to eat of his flesh before being broken on the wheel or hanged. Thousands of serfs were massacred; the terror of retaliation caused a fatal split in national unity.

Twelve years later came the decisive Hungarian "Waterloo" at a place downriver from Budapest called Mohács; a traumatic, total defeat of the Hungarian Army by the Turks, during which the king, Louis II, was drowned in a stream. Soon Buda itself was taken and the 150-year interval of Turkish occupation began. Hungary was actually split into three parts—the territory ruled by the sultan's satraps, which included the Great Plain, and much of western and southern Hungary; the rest of the west and north under Habsburg rule; and finally, Transylvania, the beautiful, wooded, mountainous province "beyond the forests," which survived for a long time, keeping an uneasy balance between Austrian and Turk under its own Hungarian princes. Here, at least, Magyar culture survived through six generations.

The Habsburgs

The liberation of Hungary came at the end of the 17th century; Buda was recaptured by the Christian forces in 1686, some three years after the vast Turkish armies were defeated under the walls of Vienna. But "liberation" simply meant exchanging one master for another. The Habsburgs turned Hungary into a province and a colony, and though the degree of oppression changed slightly during the next 150 years, the essential aim of exploiting the country for the benefit of the hereditary Habsburg lands remained the same. Before long, the first of many revolts, all of them doomed to failure, began.

The scattered resistance groups were united by Prince Ferenc Rákóczi II, the richest magnate of the country, who raised the standard of revolt in 1703. He was supported by the French, whose persistent purpose was to weaken the Habsburgs, and for eight years he and his ragged, brave troops were defiantly successful against overwhelming odds. These odds became impossible when, at the end of the War of the Spanish Succession, Vienna was able to concentrate all its forces on suppressing the Magyar fight for independence. Rákóczi ended his life in Turkish exile and the subsequent, smaller risings were usually nipped in the bud.

Slowly, Hungary's economic potential grew, though it was hampered gravely by the stubborn insistence of the nobility on its privileges, which included tax exemption and the unlimited exploitation of the peasant class. Maria Theresa (1740–80) fought a long but fruitless battle to abolish these privileges, and when she failed, found it necessary to protect the other provinces of her empire with high tariffs against Hungarian exports. This led to the country "drowning in its own fat"; in addition, the Seven Years' War demanded considerable sacrifices from the nascent middle class and the serfs. At one point, the Queen fled to the ancient Hungarian city of Pozsony (now Bratislava, in Czechoslovakia), and appealed to the chivalry of the Magyar nobles who, according to a somewhat colored version, offered their lives and blood to the young and beautiful sovereign. Maria Theresa's successor was Joseph II. He was a free-thinker and follower of Voltaire (he never had himself crowned and was nicknamed "the King in the hat") and accordingly attempted to end the prerogatives of the Hungarian nobility. But, despite the ambitiousness of his reforms and the apparent liberty behind them, he revoked the majority of them on his death bed.

Maria Theresa's Guard of Hungarian Nobles imbibed the ideas of Enlightenment, and the French Revolution also had a somewhat delayed influence. But the Hungarian Jacobins, led by the prelate Ignatius Martinovics, were betrayed and arrested, and, on May 20, 1795, put to death on the Field of Blood (Vérmező) in Budapest. Emperor Francis I and his successor, the weak-minded Ferdinand, continued the policy of repression and centralization, but the early years of the 19th century brought a great and vigorous rebirth of ideas in Hungary.

In the next decades, two men became the leaders of the struggle for reform and national independence. Their ideas were often opposed, though they were both great and true patriots of genius. To put it in a nutshell, Count István Széchenyi wanted to see Hungary first prosperous and civilized, with freedom to follow; Lajos Kossuth, his adversary, claimed that without liberty, economic progress was impossible. Széchenyi, a great Anglophile, founded the Hungarian Academy of Sciences, initiated the building of the Chain Bridge in Budapest, steamboats on the Danube and Tisza rivers, horse-racing and more scientific agriculture methods. He lost his great ideological duel with Kossuth and ended his life, after years in an asylum, by suicide.

Kossuth and Revolution

Kossuth was the first to publish regular reports about the deliberations of the Diet and, both as a political journalist and a spellbinding orator, fought indefatigably for the national cause. Imprisoned, he used his years in jail to teach himself English from Shakespeare and the Bible. The so-called Reform Age in Hungary culminated in the year of revolutions, 1848, when the February rising in Paris triggered a whole series of liberal and national explosions throughout Europe. Hungary's came on March 15, led by the students and apprentices of Pest, headed by Sándor Petőfi, the great poet, and Mór (Maurus) Jókai, destined to become the Hungarian Walter Scott. Within a few weeks, much of the past was swept away, the serfs were liberated and a responsible government was installed. But the Habsburgs would not allow Hungary even a modicum of freedom. Rousing the Slav minorities against Kossuth's government, they launched their armies against the national forces. But this led only in 1849 to the dethronement of their dynasty and Kossuth's election as regent, or governor.

The Austrians suffered a series of crushing defeats, but the young Emperor Francis Joseph and his cabinet turned to Czarist Russia for help, and the overwhelming Russian superiority in arms and men defeated the Magyar armies. Kossuth had to flee into exile with a small band of his followers. First in Turkey, later in England, France and the United States, and finally, during a long emigration in Italy (he died at the age of 92), he tried with stubborn brilliance, though with little or no success, to rally Austria's enemies to the Hungarian cause. It was, however, during these years that he elaborated a prophetic and comprehensive plan of a Danubian federation—a plan that would have solved the age-old rivalries and hostilities of the Danubian nations and still awaits realization.

The defeat of the Hungarians in their fight for independence was followed by almost two decades of Habsburg repression—executions, deportations, impressment into the Austrian forces and suppression of Magyar institutions were administered by a harsh, bureaucratic, police regime. When, in 1866, Bismarck ejected Austria from the German Reich, she had to turn eastwards. This time she sold out her Slav minorities to the Magyars; in 1867 the Hungarian liberal leader Ferenc Deák, and the ministers of Francis Joseph negotiated the *Ausgleich* (Compromise), which transformed the monarchy into a dual one.

Industrialization and economic expansion then followed, though there was constant constitutional strife and a far from liberal or sympathetic attitude towards the mass of the people and towards the large Slovak, Romanian, Serbian and Croatian minorities under Hungarian rule.

In World War I, Hungary marched with Austria and Germany, though her prime minister, Count István (Stephen) Tisza, had grave misgivings about the wisdom of such an alignment. The chauvinistic, feudalistic policies of the past decades came home to roost in 1918. There was a brief liberal revolution led by the well-meaning, but ineffective, Count Mihály (Michael) Károlyi, and Hungary broke away from Austria. Károlyi played much the same part as Kerensky did in Russia, though for a much shorter time. There followed a Communist regime under Béla Kun, which lasted 133 days; then a Romanian occupation of Budapest and finally a right-wing regime under Admiral Miklós (Nicholas) Horthy, a former aide-de-camp of Francis Joseph and the last commander of the Austro-Hungarian Navy. In the ensuing Treaty of Trianon, Hungary lost those lands inhabited by the Slovak, Romanian, Serbian and Croatian minorities as well as considerable strips of territory which were purely Hungarian; in all she was deprived of two-thirds of her former territories and 50 percent of her population.

For the next three decades she was a kingdom without a king, ruled by a regent who was an admiral without a navy, a largely peasant country in which 85 percent of the land was owned by five percent of the population: a mock-democracy in which Jewish students were restricted to five percent of the university admittances, and in which irredentist propaganda covered the misery of the over-educated and under-employed middle class. In foreign affairs, Hungary was allied to Mussolini's Italy. István Bethlen, a clever, though not too scrupulous, Transylvanian aristocrat, was premier for 10 long years, but with Hitler's rise, Hungary was drawn more and more into the German orbit, hoping to regain her lost territories through an alliance with the Nazi *Drang nach Osten*. In 1938 and 1940 this policy paid a short-term dividend, when parts of Slovakia, Yugoslavia and Transylvania were temporarily returned to Hungary.

The Scene Today

The war brought endless suffering and devastation to the country. Though Horthy tried to make a separate peace in 1944, this act only led to his arrest and the installation of an extreme rightwing, pro-Nazi Arrow Cross government. Eighty percent of Hungary's half-million Jews perished in the gas-chambers, the ghettos and the forced labor camps. The Hungarian Army was decimated in the Ukraine. Forty percent of Hungary's national wealth was destroyed before the Red Army completed its occupation on April 4, 1945, just about a month before VE Day.

The brief interval of a broad-based democratic government ended with the establishment of a People's Democracy, closely linked, economically, militarily and politically, to the Soviet Union. The Hungarian Communist Party became the ruling force under Mátyás Rákosi. Intensive industrialization, a thorough land reform and the establishment of collective farms were accompanied by a virtual reign of terror.

Stalin's death, the East Berlin rising, the Twentieth (Soviet) Party Congress, and the "Polish October" culminated in the Hungarian Revolution of 1956, which has been called both a counter-revolution (though only by the communist bloc) and a hopeless revolt against unbearable conditions. 200,000 Hungarians went into exile when it was brutally suppressed after less than two weeks, though a number have returned. János Kádár, a popular leader, has been Hungary's Party Secretary since then. Agricultural collectivization was completed in 1961, some private enterprise has been introduced into industry and commerce, and incentives have become more tangible. Today, Hungarians can once again travel abroad, though passports and foreign currency allowances are still restricted. Hungarian writers and artists are given more scope for expressing their individuality, though they must observe the party line.

Under the "New Economic Mechanism" initiated in 1968, a great many things have changed for the better. Conditions have been stimulated by the encouragement of technical and commercial initiatives, moving the economy with increasing effectiveness towards meeting consumer needs. The results are clearly visible in the well-stocked shops, new cars, better-dressed people and places of entertainment humming with activity. In the last few years, however, this economic progress has slowed noticeably and there have been considerable price increases.

In some other ways, too, things have changed. Although Hungary is still a "police state" and has the closest political and economic ties with the Soviet Union, life is becoming increasingly free; people talk and criticize more openly and no longer feel they need to look over their shoulders before telling a political joke. Hungarians are as courteous as ever and to their courtesy they have now added a sense of enjoying life, which has for many years been noticeably absent. Churches of all denominations are well-attended and relations with the Vatican have been normalized.

Contacts of all kinds with western countries increase steadily. The most striking sign of this was the return to Hungary (January 1978), by the U.S. Secretary of State Cyrus Vance, of the historic "Crown of St. Stephen," the symbol of Hungarian sovereignty, which had been handed over to American custody at the end of World War II to prevent its falling into the hands of the Russians. President Carter, in an accompanying letter, said that the act of returning the crown expressed the strengthening of the traditional friendship between the United States and Hungary.

There are more Western tourists every year, too. Great new luxury hotels, most of them built with Western capital and know-how, help to provide an atmosphere that in places could almost be taken for the West. But "almost" is the operative word, because wherever he goes the visitor will be struck by the fervent patriotic spirit of the Hungarians, influenced inevitably by recent history. These facts, surely, make this little country, perhaps more than any other, a true meeting point between West and East.

HUNGARIAN CULTURE

Talents Spread Abroad

It has been said that in the sphere of culture there are no large or small nations. All have a significant contribution to make. But the success rate of Hungarians in the world cultural scene is remarkable. Despite being imprisoned at birth behind the bars of a language which none but natives can understand properly—or perhaps because of it—Hungarian artists and writers have become outstandingly successful communicators in the fields of art and entertainment. Like some other small and intensely "national" peoples, they have emigrated with enthusiasm and transplanted extremely well; especially in Great Britain, the U.S. and France.

Literature

Medieval writers in Hungary used Latin. The first to write in the Hungarian vernacular was Bálint Balassi (1554–1594), who sang of love and war and died fighting against the Turkish invaders. It was not until the 19th century that a major work of art was produced; this was the epic drama *The Tragedy of Man* by Imre Madách (1823–1864), a strange, solitary figure. This is available in English translation, as are a few of the works of the literary trio who dominated the later 19th and early 20th centuries. They were

Mór Jókai (1825–1904), a prolific and inventive novelist; Kálmán Mikszáth (1847–1910), a campaigner for social justice whose short stories have enjoyed a revival under the present regime; and Zsigmond Móricz (1879–1942), who first depicted the misery of Hungarian peasant life.

A near contemporary of these writers, Baroness Emma Orczy, the daughter of an expatriate Hungarian nobleman, wrote only in English. Hungarians like to boast that three of their compatriots were involved in the creation of the film archetype of the English gentleman, the Scarlet Pimpernel—the Baroness wrote the books, Sir Alexander Korda produced the pictures and Leslie Howard (born Leo Steiner) played the part.

Frigyes (Frederick) Karinthy (1887–1938) was both a humorist and a satirist. His *Journey Round My Skull* is one of the several of his works to have been published in English.

Modern Authors

Among Hungarian writers living and working abroad, the late Arthur Koestler (1905–1983) won a world-wide reputation, both with his novels and his philosophical and popular scientific books, ranging from *Darkness at Noon* to *Scum of the Earth,* from *The Yogi and the Commissar* to in-depth exploration of humor, creativity, biology and the space-age.

One must mention Áron Tamási (1897–1966), the poet-novelist of Transylvania, whose almost untranslatable, richly-embroidered prose is like the ornate Székely embroideries of his native land. Tibor Déry (1894–1977) wrote among other English-translated works a classic short story, *Niki.* Prominent among contemporary novelists are the erudite and aristocratic Péter Esterházy (*Production Novel 1979*) and George Konrád whose recent *The Loser* (published in English) is a Magyar *Good Soldier Schweik.*

Among authors very popular in Hungary today are the dramatist István Örkény (1912–1979), best known perhaps for his piece "Cats' Play," and the novelists Géza Ottlik, Zoltán Jékely and Miklós Mészöly.

A Poetic Sweep

If you visit Hungary, you will inevitably hear a great deal about poets past and present—and rightly so. They were great and tragic figures. The three greatest—Sándor Petőfi, Endre Ady and Attila József—all died young; Petőfi in battle, Ady of a blood disease, József by suicide.

There had been many considerable poets in Hungary during the 18th century, but a sudden, new blossoming of poetry, a great resurgence, came in the 1820s. Mihály (Michael) Vörösmarty (1800–55), the first great Hungarian epic poet, delved into his nation's past and described the heroic deeds in rolling hexameters.

His translations of Shakespeare's *Julius Caesar* and *King Lear* were particularly brilliant. In János Arany (1817–82) the epic qualities of Hungarian poetry reached their highest fulfilment. As a translator—in Hungary a profession rated as highly as poet—Arany gave his nation the best of all foreign-language versions of *Hamlet.*

Sándor Petőfi (1823–49), Hungary's most original poet, fulfilled the ideal fate of a burning, restless soul, a patriot and a prophet. At the age of 26 he disappeared in the battle of Segesvár, where the veteran Polish General Bem, who had joined Kossuth, was trying to check the Russian armies. Petőfi's life was short and violent, full of love and hate, triumph and defeat; he was a comet, drawing a fiery trail across the heavens and then vanishing suddenly. His heritage has been inexhaustible and has again and again inspired his country's poets.

Between Petőfi's death and the début of Endre Ady (1877–1919) there were a great many good poets in Hungary—but no great ones. But when Ady arrived, he became the leader of a new renaissance, an almost feverish flowering of Hungarian poetry. He headed the literary group that had founded the important magazine *Nyugat* (West)—a group to which most of the leading writers belonged for the next two generations. This single word marked their aims—to turn to the West instead of the East; to fuse modern Western culture with the traditional heritage of Hungarian poetry.

Attila József

Even the scantiest survey of Hungarian poetry would be incomplete without four final names. Attila József (1905–37) came from a proletarian family—his mother was a washerwoman. A rebel who joined the Communist Party only to be expelled; a lover of the good things of life who dreamed in vain on a monthly pittance—he was only 32 when he threw himself in front of a train on the shores of Lake Balaton. He was the most intellectual of poets.

Miklós Radnóti (1909–44) was a very learned yet lyrical poet, who was murdered by a Nazi guard after enduring every possible torture and indignity in a death march to a concentration camp. His final poems, written during his slave labor service and in the last weeks of his life, were miraculously preserved and represent a terrible indictment of man's inhumanity to man.

Sándor Weöres is the great eclectician of Hungary; a virtuoso of form and thought, he is always experimenting, often hermetic, burningly sensuous and yet child-like in flashes of simplicity.

Gyula Illyés, winner of the Grand Prix de Poésie, died in 1983. Born in 1902 of simple peasant stock, he imbibed the riches of Latin, and especially French, culture and lived to become the doyen of Hungarian poets. His prose was just as vivid as his sensuously beautiful poems. There are translations in English of much he has written, including his most famous prose work *The People of the Puszta.*

Other poets worthy of mention are the Catholic János Pilinszky (1921–81), Lőrinc Szabó, István Vas, László Nagy and Ferenc Juhász.

English-language selections of the above authors' works occasionally appear in anthologies and in publications from Budapest. If you need reminders of the unfamiliar names, look around you! The streets and squares of Budapest bear the names of all her favorite men and women of letters.

Music

When St. Gellért (Gerard), the first Bishop of Hungary, came to the country almost 1,000 years ago, he rested at a small inn. In the evening he went to bed early, but could not sleep, for outside in the garden a maid was pounding grain and singing. "The sweet melody of the Magyars," St. Gellért said, and listened intently. Ever since then, "the sweet melody of the Magyars," though often polluted by the meretricious, has been a constant source of inspiration for Hungarian musicians. Hungarians and violins seem to have been created for one another and the Magyar recruiting dance, the *verbunkos* (from the German word *Werbung,* recruitment) found its way into Beethoven's *Eroica* and Mozart's A-major Violin Concerto; just as the fiery *Rákóczi March* became an integral part of Berlioz' *Damnation of Faust.* Great foreign musicians often came to Hungary—Beethoven and Hummel gave concerts in Buda, and Haydn was for many years the conductor of Prince Esterházy's private orchestra.

Ferenc Erkel (1810–93) created Hungarian opera. His earliest works are forgotten now, but in their day—the 1840s—they were as excitedly proclaimed as those of Verdi in Italy, and for similar reasons: they encouraged nationalistic sentiment. *Bánk Bán,* which came later (1861), has stood the test of political fluctuations and is still given an airing in Budapest on national day. Erkel was equally famous as a pianist and conductor. He founded the Budapest Philharmonic Orchestra and was musical director of the National Theater.

The opera composer of greatest repute abroad was Carl Goldmark (1830–1915), although of his numerous tuneful works only one, *The Queen of Sheba,* remains in the international repertoire. But in the last two decades a startling musical innovator called György Ligeti (born 1923) has burst on the scene and achieved critical acclaim worldwide with his "micropolyphonic" compositions in which he employs primitive instruments—telephone bells, motor horns and electronic gadgets—to move masses of sound about. *Glissandi, Articulation,* and *Clocks and Clouds* are among his most interesting choral-orchestral works. In 1978 came his first opera, *Le Grand Macabre,* immediately recognized as a musical event in musical history. Ligeti may never be performed in the puritanical atmosphere of his native land, but he is a cult figure in Germany, Scandinavia and Britain.

Ferenc (Franz) Liszt (1811–86) has often been claimed by Germany, but when, at the age of eleven, he had his first public concert in Buda (before setting off on a foreign tour), he announced: "I am a Hungarian and I cannot imagine any greater happiness than to offer the first fruits of my training and study to my beloved country"—an unequivocal declaration. Liszt, of course, was not only a great composer but an even greater virtuoso. Though he spent most of his life abroad, he never severed his connections with his native country. He became the first director of the Budapest Academy of Music. His *Hungarian Rhapsodies,* of which he composed 20, and the symphonic poem *Hungaria* proved his unbroken links with the soil that reared him.

Jenő Hubay and Ernő Dohnányi have both been composers of talent and brilliant performers—Hubay on the violin and Dohnányi on the piano.

The two modern Hungarian composers who have found world fame, Béla Bartók (1881–1945) and Zoltán Kodály (1882–1967), have both gone back to the deepest roots of folk music. They explored small villages and tiny settlements, making records of the peasant songs.

Bartók, who spent his last years in the United States, tried to create an independent language of music on the basis of ancient East European folk music. His ballets, *The Wooden Prince* and *The Miraculous Mandarin,* show a demonic imagination creating organic life and perfect form; his one-act opera, *Duke Bluebeard's Castle,* his *Cantata Profana* and his amazingly intricate chamber music have earned him a place as the fourth 'B' with the three other geniuses—Bach, Beethoven and Brahms.

Zoltán Kodály's music was perhaps the first in Hungary to merge East and West in a passionate, beautiful union. Kodály was less of a revolutionary than Bartók, as he was often looking into the past. His *Psalmus Hungaricus,* first performed in 1923, composed to the words of a 16th-century poet, with a tenor solo, mixed choir and orchestra, immediately became world famous. It was followed by his folk opera *Háry János,* by his *Dances of Galanta* and his *Te Deum of Budavár,* all equally successful. But Kodály, above all, was the master of composing for the human voice, and especially for children. His method of teaching young people to sing is still used in Hungary and abroad.

Music-Makers of Today

Among modern Hungarian composers one may also briefly mention Ferenc (Francis) Szabó for his chamber music; László Lajtha for his research into folk themes; Leó Weiner for his research into folk music, and György Ránki, who also sought inspiration in Hungarian folk tales. Other well-known composers are György Kurtág and Attila Bozay. A number of young pianists, among them Zoltán Kocsis and Dezső Ránki, are achieving fame far beyond the borders of Hungary.

A very important group of Hungarian musicians lives outside Hungary. Many of them are indeed household names. Sir Georg Solti has been in charge of many famous orchestras, including the Chicago Symphony Orchestra, Covent Garden and the Paris Opera. Two other Georges, György (George) Sebestyén and George Széll, also belong to the major ambulant conductors of our age. Antal Doráti has been commuting for years between Europe and America—and there are many more.

The late Joseph Szigeti has been acclaimed as one of the greatest violinists of all times. Among contemporary virtuosos, Andor Földes, Tamás Vásáry, and Péter Frankl are celebrated names.

Nor have Hungarians lacked eminence in light music. Franz Lehár was a Hungarian and his *Merry Widow* has proved truly immortal. So were Imre Kálmán, Pál Ábrahám and Miklós Brodszky, whose operettas and musical comedies have filled many a theater for years on end. Hungarians have also contributed to international jazz festivals; the pianist Attila Garay, the contrabassist Aladár Pege and the drummer Gyula Kovács (whom American jazz critics have hailed as the best in Europe) are masters of their modern art.

When summer comes to Hungary the sound of music does not die away. Under the stars, within the walls and parks of old palaces and abbeys, choral and orchestral concerts draw large crowds: Beethoven at Martonvásár, Haydn at Fertőd, organ recitals and medieval court music at Tihany and Buda castle, chamber concerts at Keszthely . . . musical picnics of an elegant kind.

Art and Architecture

Successive invasions, the long Turkish occupation and the numerous battles that raged on her soil have left few ancient Hungarian monuments and buildings standing. Nor have Hungarian architects been particularly brilliant; the cathedrals and palaces, the fortresses and magnates' mansions were usually designed and built by foreigners. The great building boom of the last decades of the 19th century produced an eclectic, bastard style, with an almost pathological passion for cupolas; the results can still be seen in Budapest and most provincial cities. The chief exception to this rule was Ödön Lechner (1845–1914), who created a new, short-lived "Hungarian Art Nouveau" style, perhaps best exemplified by the former Hungarian Foreign Trade Bank in Budapest, in Rosenberg Házaspár Utca, not far from the Parliament.

For the most striking modern buildings, such as the circular Hotel Budapest, foreign architects are again responsible. But two names of native significance are those of Marcell Breuer (1902–81) and József Finta (born 1935), today Hungary's best-known architect, who designed many of the large new hotels in the country.

Hungarian sculpture has had its academic representatives of neo-Baroque, among them Zsigmond Kisfaludi Strobl (1884–1975), responsible for the massive Liberation Monument on Gellért Hill, Imre Varga (born 1903), István Kiss (born 1927), and the talented Ferenc Medgyessy (1881–1958), who also followed classical precedents.

Outside Hungary, the best-known Hungarian painter is the ambitious and talented Philip de László (1869–1937), Europe's most fashionable portraitist between the wars. Inside Hungary, no school of original painting developed. Her best domestic artists followed in the train of the French masters. Pál Szinyei Merse's (1845–1920) *Picnic in May* and *Lady in Violet,* which have pride of place in Budapest's National Gallery, derive from Manet. The naïf surrealism of Tivadar Csontváry Kosztka (1853–1919) is best seen at Pécs. Jézsef Rippl-Rónai (1861–1927) introduced his fellow-countrymen to Parisian art-nouveau. As in other artistic fields, Hungarian painters, sculptors and illustrators have scattered all over the world: the highly idiosyncratic art of Vasarely (Vásárhelyi), to name but one, is now known worldwide. Other well-known names are those of the sculptor Amerigo Tot (Imre Tóth, 1909–84), Belá Kindor (1931–72) and Lajos Guláçsy (1882–1932). Lajos Kassák (1887–1967), poet, painter and essayist, was the prophet of the Hungarian avant-garde who tried to establish contacts between this and the international avant-garde movement. He was a controversial figure, only "rehabilitated" after his death. László Moholy-Nagy (1895–1946) was an outstanding personality of the international avant-garde and a leading light of the Bauhaus at Dessau; he worked out a system of teaching the appreciation of visual arts. He died abroad.

The Hungarian National Gallery in Budapest has the best collection of native artists. The Fine Arts Museum contains some celebrated Italian, Flemish and Spanish artists. Beautiful relics of ecclesiastical art are kept at the Christian Museum in Esztergom and in the Serbian Orthodox Collection at Szentendre.

Horror Masks and Brandy Flasks

Delightful combinations of the strands which make up the national artistic temperament—gypsy, Oriental, Teutonic, Slav, classical—occur in the applied arts and crafts. Peasant traditions are powerful and idiosyncratic. Artistically the Hungarians are not all that creative; but they have enormous talent for improvization, decoration and ingenious contrivances (of the last-named, the Rubik cube is the latest novelty). The Museum of Applied Arts in Budapest is a fascinating compendium of artefacts with the inimitable Magyar stamp.

Cultural shocks await the visitor to Hungary wherever local arts and crafts are strong: in the popular openair village museums or *skanzen;* in the flower-painted town of Kalocsa, where the rich botany of the Danube meadows is reproduced all over the cottage facades; in the "horror" masks of the Carnival procession at Mohács; in the clusters of ceramic fountain statuary at Pécs. . . . ceramics are the glory of Hungarian craftwork, milestones on its folk history.

The earliest pottery dates from the 9th century. Progressive improvements in techniques led to the introduction of glazes, at first on insides and rims, afterwards overall. From the 16th century, when much of Hungary was under Ottoman rule, the simple bird-and-flower patterns became more Oriental and geometrical. Famous, too, is Hungarian handmade lace.

In the more peaceful atmosphere of the 17th century a new era began. Craftsmen settled into village communities and organized their guilds. Hungary expanded into an empire, with many foreign trading links, and this greatly benefited her potters. Ceramics of that period are highly decorative, with "slip trailing" as the predominant technique. Ropes of "slip," a colored liquid clay, were squeezed on to the surface of the damp pot, producing a slightly raised pattern, and the colors, usually green, brown and black, were seen through a transparent glaze. Later, in the interests of speedier production, the brush superseded the "trailer," giving a flatter design.

Traditional forms, apart from common plates and dishes, were variations on the conventional bottle and pitcher shapes. Water vessels, the *korsó* with narrow neck and the *kanta* with a wide one, were often unglazed—the slow evaporation of the contents through the porous clay kept the liquids cool.

The *kulacs,* the pilgrim's brandy flask, has small feet and small handles, which allowed it to be stood upright or slung from a shoulderstrap. The *pereckulacs* is ring-shaped, with a hole in the middle. Brandy flasks also exist in the shape of little kegs and plum stones. Most pieces have an inscription incised in the clay—the owner's name, or a poem, or a guild symbol. Many beautiful examples can be seen at the Ethnographical Museum in Budapest and the Déri Museum at Debrecen.

The folk-art of pottery flourishes still. Many potters work in country districts in the traditional idiom; a few hold the coveted title of "Master of Folk Art." The Hungarian potter best-known abroad is Margit Kovács (1902–1977), famous for her bizarre little groups and figurines.

Stage and Screen

In no other field of creative endeavor have Hungarians been as prominent as in the cinema and in the theater. A large number of the Hollywood "giants" were Hungarians. Adolph Zukor's long life-span covered practically the whole history of the movies; and on the Paramount lot, there is still a signpost showing the exact distance to the tiny Hungarian village where he was born. The Fox in Twentieth Century Fox was William Fox (Fuchs), a Hungarian. We have already mentioned Sir Alexander Korda, who was for long a vital prop of the British film industry and whose screen-hits would fill pages. His two brothers, Zoltan and Vincent, were his constant collaborators, Zoltan as director and Vincent as set-designer. Their lives have been entertainingly described in the recent book *Charmed Lives* by Michael Korda.

Nor has there been a lack of Hungarian filmstars—though some of them have completely sloughed off their Magyar skins. Paul Lukas and Peter Lorre, genuine Hollywood stalwarts, Tony Curtis (born Bernie Schwarz), Cornel Wilde, "Cuddles" Sakall, Zsa-Zsa Gabor and her sister and many others have been part of the Hollywood scene.

Hungary has always been a theater-loving country and Budapest has more theaters than Broadway; but Hungarian playwrights have been less successful in New York and London than on the European continent. The big name in this field is that of Ferenc Molnár (1878–1952), a poet of the theater, a writer of wicked wit and cheerful cynicism whose plays usually center on the eternal battle of the sexes in a raffish, sophisticated society. *The Guardsman* and *Liliom* are 20th-century classics and often performed in English.

There have been others to share the limelight since Molnár. Melchior Lengyel (1880–1974) is best-known for two such opposite achievements as the story of *Ninotchka* and the libretto of Bartók's *The Miraculous Mandarin*.

One of the Hungarian cinema's chief representatives is Miklós Jancsó, whose main preoccupation is with guilt and courage. His austere and moving films have achieved world acceptance. There are echoes of Dreyer and Bergman in his work, but he has a style and philosophy all his own. Other outstanding Hungarian film directors are András Kovács, Zoltán Fabry, Károly Makk, György Révész, István Szabó (who won an Oscar in 1982 for his film *Mephisto*), Istvan Gáal, Pal Sándor and Márta Mészáros. Pal Sándor (born 1939) is making his name in the West for the beautiful films he builds round crucial historical events. *Improperly Dressed* (1978) concerned abortive Communist risings in 1919; *Deliver Us From Evil* (1980) portrayed the siege of Budapest in 1944; *Football of the Good Old Days* (1981) was about Hungarian Jews in the 1930s; and *Daniel Takes a Train* (1984) dealt with the 1956 uprising. Hungary's latest international film success is István Szabó's *Colonel Redl,* an evocative portrayal of military life under the Austro-Hungarian monarchy.

Despite the increasing spread of television, the cinema flourishes and more than 4,000 performances are given nightly up and down the land. Hungary still awaits the arrival of her own movie classic, but official attitudes are more liberal now and the time will soon be ripe. Meanwhile, the visitor can always take advantage of amazingly cheap seats and may even see, especially on television, the occasional western.

HUNGARIAN FOOD AND DRINK

From Gulyas to Dobostorta

Hungarian cooking is a sophisticated and delicious anthology of color, shape, odor and taste. It has absorbed, though with suitable modifications, the best of Viennese, French, Serbian and Oriental traditions. There have been some unjust generalizations about its being too spicy or too heavy. This may be true in some parts of the country, but certainly not in Budapest or other culinary centers.

From Soup to Soup

Hungarian soups are memorable experiences. Perhaps the most fabulous is the Magyar version of *bouillabaisse.* It is called *halászlé* and is best eaten in Szeged or on Lake Balaton, though most Budapest restaurants also serve it. The Szeged version is a thick, rich soup made from giant catfish, carp or sterlet. The Balaton *halászlé* is a clear soup that contains onions, a moderate amount of paprika and is made with bream, pike-perch or shad. In many places cubed potatoes are added and sometimes small pieces of *pasta* (gnocchi-like bits of dough, kneaded with egg) are used to make the mixture richer. There is only one caveat—beware of the bones!

Goulash or *gulyás* is the Hungarian dish that is best known internationally, but in most cases when it is served outside the country, it is not goulash at all. A proper *gulyás* is a soup, though a soup that can be a meal in itself. It will contain slices of green pepper, as well as paprika, tomatoes, onions, *csipetke* (little dumplings) and enough rich gravy to make it completely liquid. Of course, its main ingredient will be pieces of beef (or occasionally pork). Contrary to popular misconceptions, it is not hideously spicy, does not contain any sour cream and is never served with rice. It does sometimes number caraway seeds among its many ingredients.

Other Hungarian soups include a modified version of the Russian cabbage soup known as *káposztaleves*. Particularly good on winter days is *bableves,* made from broad beans and lightly flavored with paprika and with boiled ham, bacon or sausages floating in it. A delicious, non-spicy but tasty soup is *Ujházi tyúkhúsleves,* a chicken broth which is served together with the meat and vegetables cooked with it. Other very popular soups include potato soup, *lebbencsleves* (a broth containing pieces of pasta and red pepper and shreds of fried bacon) and *húsleves* (bouillon), with or without a raw egg. Delicious in the summer is *meggyleves,* made from morello cherries and sour cream and chilled to an agreeably cooling temperature.

Main Courses

What *we* think of as goulash—a paprika-flavored stew in which meat predominates—is known in Hungary as *pörkölt* or *tokány.* This can contain almost any kind of meat or fowl, though mutton and lamb are on the whole rarely eaten in Budapest, though more frequently in the provinces. It consists of much the same ingredients as the *gulyás* we have referred to, but it is a solid dish and is usually served with sour cream and one of the many variants of dumplings; it is usually accompanied by a cucumber or lettuce salad. A regional variation of this theme is the so-called *székelygulyás,* which originated in Transylvania. It is a tasty combination of cabbage, sour cream, paprika and meat, usually pork. This, of course, is a main dish. As an alternative, you might try *kolozsvári rakottkáposzta* (layered cabbage); this is a very filling dish of sour cabbage, eggs, rice, smoked sausage and pork.

Among the other typical dishes you will find in Hungary are various stuffed vegetables. For instance, *töltött paprika,* green peppers filled with minced (ground) meat and served in a rich tomato sauce, and *töltött káposzta,* cabbage leaves similarly prepared. There is also *serpenyős rostélyos,* which is made from sirloin steaks with onions, paprika and potatoes. Even the Hungarian versions of such international dishes as *Wiener Schnitzel*—in Hungarian, *bécsi szelet*—have a surprising and delightful taste of their own.

A favorite meat dish is the *fatányéros* (wooden platter), the Hungarian version of a mixed grill, surrounded by small helpings of salads, vegetables and crowned with bacon.

There is a great variety of excellent freshwater fish in the country—the giant catfish of the Danube, the *fogas* (pike-perch) of the Balaton, and its young, the *süllő,* one of Hungary's greatest delicacies, the sterlet of the Tisza and the mirror carp. One of the finest fish courses is the *rácponty* (devilled carp) with potatoes, peppers, tomatoes and onions, topped with sour cream.

Turkey is particularly good in Hungary, but chickens, geese and ducks are equally luscious and tasty. *Paprikás csirke* (paprika chicken) is usually served with sour cream poured over it and a side dish of cucumber salad. *Galuska* (small dumplings boiled in water) adds an additional attraction to the rich, golden-red gravy. *Rántott csirke* is the Hungarian version of Southern fried chicken.

Finishing the Meal in Style

Few countries have such variety and enchanting perfection in boiled desserts and cakes. *Túrós csusza* is made of small strips of *pasta* spread with curd cheese, sour cream and scraps of pork crackling. *Barátfüle* (literally, friar's ears) are, in effect, jam pockets and use the same *pasta* as *túrós csusza.* For extra sophistication they are sprinkled with ground nuts.

Hungarian noodles are called *metélt* or *nudli.* They are sprinkled with ham pieces, nuts, or poppy seeds mixed with sugar. The Hungarian pancakes *(palacsinta)* are equally tasty—their fillings can be sweetened curd cheese with raisins, ground walnuts, chocolate, various kinds of jam or poppy seeds.

Hungarian pastry is one of the most varied and tempting in the world, and can be readily sampled in any *cukrászda* (pastry shop). Perhaps the most famous is the *rétes* (the Austrian strudel), a paper-thin flaky pastry, which is filled with fruits, ground nuts, poppy seeds—even sweetened curd cheese and peppered cabbage. The *dobostorta,* a layered fancy cake with a hard burnt sugar top, is widely imitated throughout the world.

Hungarian cheeses include *pálpusztai,* which is not unlike gorgonzola, a *bakony,* which resembles camembert; an unusual cream cheese is *körözött,* a mixture of ewe cheese, butter, paprika and caraway seeds.

What to Drink

After some difficult years, Hungarian vintages have returned to their former excellence. A few of the most famous include: *Tokaji aszú* (Tokay), a dessert wine almost like a sweet, but heartwarming, brandy; *Egri bikavér,* the famous Bull's Blood from Eger (a full-bodied Burgundy); other fine red wines are *Medoc Noir,* also from the Eger district, *Szekszárdi* and *Soproni kékfrankos,* from southern and western Hungary respectively. Among white wines are *Badacsonyi kéknyelű* (moderately dry) and *Badacsonyi szürkebarát* (sweet), both from the sunny slopes of the long-extinct volcano overlooking the northern shore of Lake Balaton. *Debrői hárslevelű* is an extremely popular white wine from the famous wine district of Gyöngyös. From the extreme south of Hungary come *Villányi hárslevelü* (white) and *burgundi* (red).

There are also large vineyards in the Great Plain, around the area of Kecskemét. Hungarian *barack,* the apricot brandy, is smooth and has a deceptively mild effect, with a fiery aftermath you will remember and wish to experience again. There are other Hungarian liqueurs made from plums, pears, cherries and even green walnuts.

For those who prefer not to drink wine with their meals there is an excellent choice of natural mineral waters. Then there are several popular native brands of beer, the best known probably being *Kőbányai világos.* Foreign beers, such as Pilsen, and other Czech, as well as Austrian and East and West German, beers are also freely available, while the well-known Danish *Tuborg* lager is produced in Hungary under license. Various brands of canned beer are also on sale. Both Coca Cola and Pepsi Cola are to be found everywhere. The coffee at breakfast, which was at one time something to be avoided in all but the best hotels, is now excellent almost everywhere; so is the *espresso* coffee, which Hungarians drink in large quantities. Tea, alas, is usually brought to you in the form of a tea bag and not-quite-boiling water.

EXPLORING
HUNGARY

BUDAPEST

The Cosmopolitan City

There are many ways to know a city, varying degrees of discovering its essence. You can form a picture of London by visiting Soho, Chelsea and Westminster; you can claim that you know the Paris of Montmartre, Montparnasse and the Faubourg St Honoré or the Vienna of the Naschmarkt, Kärntnerstrasse and the Heuriger—but every capital has many faces, and Budapest is no exception. Twice-battered within 12 years, some houses still pockmarked with bullet-holes, the constant chaos of building and rebuilding enveloping many quarters, you will find in it light and shadow, moving beauty and stark ugliness, baroque elegance and modern utility. But it has also a spirit of its own, a unique blend of *laissez-faire,* biting wit and self-deprecation, cattiness and soaring enthusiasm, ribaldry and hearts-and-flowers sentiment. Hungarians are very articulate indeed, and their nimble tongues leave few secrets untold. Budapest has over two million inhabitants, about 20 percent of the population of the whole country, but news travels amazingly quickly and private affairs seldom remain private for long.

Cities are living beings and sometimes they change so quickly that you barely take eyes off them before finding them totally altered. Budapest is no exception, but here the changes have been forced upon a city that has one of the loveliest situations in Europe, straddling, as it does, one of Europe's most majestic rivers. Both

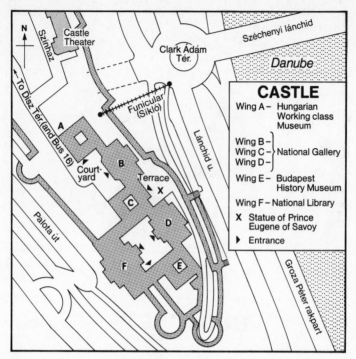

in 1944–45 and in 1956 there was prolonged street fighting within
its limits and, as a result of this and of the innumerable battles,
sieges and civil wars of earlier centuries, there is not a great deal
of distinguished architecture in the city; but there are small details,
unexpected corners, sudden delights that reward the pedestrian.
It is not a city that you can explore properly in a car. The distances
are modest; the more reason to stroll—and to linger.

Castle Hill

Start by taking a taxi or a bus (no. 16 from Engels Tér) up to
Castle Hill. Here, around the former royal palace, a true labor of
love has been performed. The seven-week siege of 1944–45 turned
the whole district into a vast acreage of ruins. The final German
stand was made in the palace itself, which was burnt out completely, its walls largely reduced to rubble, with a few scarred pillars
and fire-blackened statues sticking out of the devastation. The destruction was incalculable—yet not without unexpected advan-
tages. Archeologists and art historians were provided with a unique
opportunity to explore the past, to discover the medieval buildings
that had once stood on the site of the Baroque and neo-Baroque
palace. The details of the edifices of the kings of the Árpád and
Anjou dynasties, of the Holy Roman Emperor Sigismund, and of
the great national king, Matthias Corvinus, have been preserved

in about 80 different reports, travelogues, books and itineraries, which spoke with the authenticity and appreciation of contemporaries about the beauty and riches of the Buda royal residence.

The post-1945 rebuilding was slow and elaborately considerate—it tried to restore and enhance the values of the different epochs in their historic and architectural beauty. In some places more than six meters (20 ft.) of rubble had to be removed, and the remains found on the medieval levels were restored on the original planes. The foundation walls and the medieval castle-walls freed from the tall mounds of rubble were completed and the ramparts surrounding the medieval royal residence were erected again as close to their original shape and size as possible.

The whole Castle Hill area is now banned to private cars, except for those of residents and guests at the Hilton Hotel. Taxis are allowed, as is the no. 16 bus, which now runs more frequently.

The former Royal Palace itself can be reached in a few minutes on foot from Dísz Tér (Square), where you leave your bus or taxi, or for 10 Ft. you can take the funicular (cable) railway, known as the "Sikló," from the square at the western end of the Chain Bridge, Clark Ádám Tér, to Szent György Tér (St. George's Square), a few yards from the northern entrance to the Palace. In front of the Palace, facing the Danube, stands an equestrian statue of Prince Eugene of Savoy, one of the commanders of the army fighting the Turks at the end of the 17th century. From the terrace on which the statue stands there is a superb view over Pest, on the opposite bank. The Palace has been restored to its original splendor and is now a vast museum complex and cultural center. In the northern wing is the Museum of the Hungarian Working Class Movement—here are relics from guilds and from the beginnings of modern industry, as well as an exhibition of Socialist Art in Hungary. The immense center block contains the Hungarian National Gallery, with a wide-ranging collection of Hungarian fine arts throughout the ages, from medieval ecclesiastical paintings and statues to works of the 19th and 20th centuries, which are richly represented. Visitors should especially note the works of the Romantic painter Munkacsy, the Impressionist Szinyei Merse and the neo-Surrealist Csontváry Kosztka. There is also a large collection of modern Hungarian sculpture. The southern block contains the Budapesti Történeti Muzeum (Budapest History Museum), which has a permanent exhibition entitled "1,000 Years of Our Capital" which depicts through historical documents and exhibits the medieval history and art of Buda fortress and of the capital as a whole. The beautifully restored Medieval Hall of the Knights is particularly impressive. The western block is the home of the National Library, with over five million volumes.

The whole of Castle Hill, a long narrow plateau with several streets of miniature palaces and mansions and a few medieval churches, saw bitter fighting in 1944–45, but restoration work is virtually complete. The great "Coronation Church" or Matthias Church (Mátyás templom), officially the Church of Our Lady, has been rebuilt and refurnished. Dating back to the middle of the 13th century, it has suffered many changes and attacks—for almost a century and a half, it was the principal mosque of the Turkish overlords. It was badly damaged in the recapture of Buda in 1686, and was completely reconstructed at the end of the 19th century, receiving an asymmetrical west front with one high and one low spire, and a fine rose window. The south porch is 14th century, and inside there are a number of paintings and sculptures of considerable age and artistic value. The *encolpium*—an enameled casket, containing a miniature copy of the gospel, to be worn on the chest—belonging to King Béla III (1173–1196) and his wife, Anne of Châtillon, is of particular interest; the burial crowns of the royal couple and a cross, scepter and rings found in their excavated graves are to be seen here, too. The Treasury contains Renaissance and Baroque chalices, monstrances and vestments. High Mass is celebrated here at 10 A.M. on Sundays, with a fine orchestra and choir; get there early if you want a seat. It was in this church that the last two kings of Hungary, Franz Josef and Charles, were crowned.

Outside the church there is a richly convoluted Baroque column dedicated to the Trinity. Nearby are the remains of the oldest church of Castle Hill, built by Dominican friars in the 13th century; only the tower and one wall have survived and these have, with considerable skill, been incorporated in to the impressive Hilton Hotel, which manages to combine old and new architecture to form a harmonious whole. Close at hand is the modern Romanesque Halászbástya (Fishermen's Bastion), which consists of cloisters of white stone whose columns and arches provide perfect frames for the splendid view below. The top is crowned by a round tower, which houses a highly-popular cafe-restaurant; in front stands a modern bronze equestrian statue of St. Stephen, Hungary's first king.

The town houses that line the narrow streets of Castle Hill are now occupied by offices, restaurants and a few lucky foreign diplomats. In András Hess Square, named after the first Hungarian printer (who started work in 1473), there is the famous Vörös Sün (House of the Red Hedgehog), formerly an inn and now a snack bar. Throughout Castle Hill, houses of varying historical styles stand cheek by jowl. At no. 9 Táncsics Mihály Street a Baroque building masks the dungeons where Lajos Kossuth, Hungary's great national leader, spent more than three years in prison; next door (no. 7) Beethoven stayed in 1800 when he came to Buda to conduct his works. It now houses the Museum of Music History. Also fascinating are the Museum of Hungarian Trade and Catering at no. 4 Fortuna Utca, and the Golden Eagle Pharmacy Museum at no. 18 Tarnok Utca. To the north, in Kapisztrán Tér (Square of St. John Capistrano) is all that remains of the Gothic church of St. Mary Magdalene—the tower, which has been carefully restored.

Narrow medieval alleyways connect the main streets of Castle Hill, and in almost each of them there is something of historical interest. There are fine Gothic buildings in Úri Street, which also contains the grave of Abdurrahman Ali, the last Turkish pasha to rule Buda. The buildings towards the southern end of the Hill include the recently-rebuilt Castle Theater, where Beethoven once performed. While it retains its original facade, the interior has been planned in accordance with the most modern principles.

Down to the Danube

Then you can start your descent towards the Danube. There are many winding paths and roads, but the easiest leads south to the ancient quarter called the Tabán. Though most of the small, sunken houses have been demolished—many in the interests of traffic—here and there a few picturesque buildings remain. At no. 1 Apród Street is the house where Ignác Semmelweis, the great Hungarian physician and the discoverer of the cause of childbed fever, was born in 1818. This is now a museum of medical history, worth a visit for the Baroque building alone. Some way upstream, the other side of Clark Ádám Tér (Adam Clark Square) in the narrow strip between Castle Hill and the Danube, much of the ambience of Old Buda is preserved, though the old houses are being demolished. A broad promenade flanks the river embankment and a single street runs parallel with it. The cross-streets all climb the hill, some of them flights of steps rather like the old streets of Montmartre. Fő (Main) Street starts at the Chain Bridge, where a square has been named after the British builder of the bridge, Adam Clark. At the northern end of Fő Street there is a bronze statue of Joseph Bem, the Polish general who led one of the main Hungarian armies in the struggle for freedom in 1848–49. It was at this statue that a great demonstration was held in 1956 in sympathy with the Polish striving for liberal reform—the demonstration which developed into the great and tragic Hungarian uprising.

One of the relics of the Turkish occupation is in the nearby Mecset (Mosque) Street—the tomb or *türbe* of Gül Baba, the "Father of the Roses," a Dervish and poet. His tomb, built of carved stone blocks with four oval windows, was a place of pilgrimage for several centuries, even after the Turks had been ejected from Hungary.

To the south of Castle Hill rises Gellért Hill. It's only 232 meters (770 ft.) high, but from its summit the whole city appears spread out like an unrolling tapestry. Looking down from the hill, which bears an old fortress on its rocky crown, the scenic panorama of one of the most spectacularly-chosen city sites spreads to the horizon. Directly opposite is the vast plain occupied by Pest, the more modern part of the twin city. Spreading on the left or eastern bank

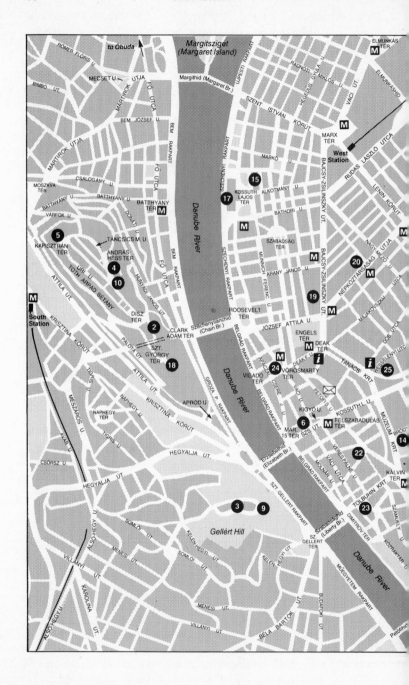

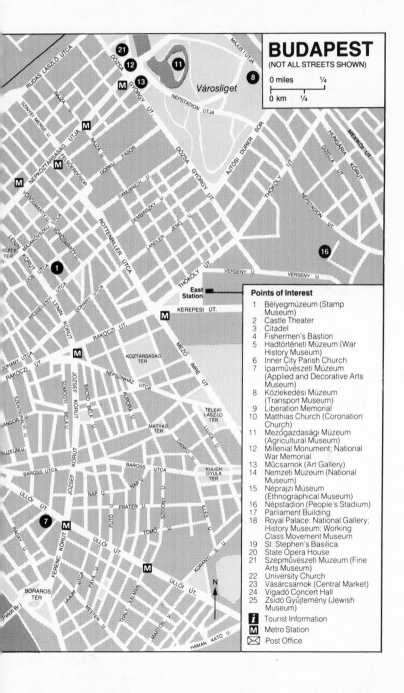

BUDAPEST
(NOT ALL STREETS SHOWN)

0 miles   ¼
0 km   ¼

Városliget

Points of Interest

1 Bélyegmúzeum (Stamp Museum)
2 Castle Theater
3 Citadel
4 Fishermen's Bastion
5 Hadtörténeti Múzeum (War History Museum)
6 Inner City Parish Church
7 Iparművészeti Múzeum (Applied and Decorative Arts Museum)
8 Közlekedési Múzeum (Transport Museum)
9 Liberation Memorial
10 Matthias Church (Coronation Church)
11 Mezőgazdasági Múzeum (Agricultural Museum)
12 Millenial Monument; National War Memorial
13 Műcsarnok (Art Gallery)
14 Nemzeti Múzeum (National Museum)
15 Néprajzi Múseum (Ethnographical Museum)
16 Népstadion (People's Stadium)
17 Parliament Building
18 Royal Palace: National Gallery; History Museum; Working Class Movement Museum
19 St. Stephen's Basilica
20 State Opera House
21 Szépművészeti Múzeum (Fine Arts Museum)
22 University Church
23 Vásárcsarnok (Central Market)
24 Vigadó Concert Hall
25 Zsidó Gyűjtemény (Jewish Museum)

i Tourist Information
M Metro Station
✉ Post Office

of the Danube, the vista is closed by the towering apartment blocks of the distant industrial suburbs. Between the labyrinth of roofs, domes, and spires, it is possible to discern the inner and outer boulevards, the large green oases of the many parks and the occasional squares.

The Danube itself curves through the capital roughly from north to south, dividing repeatedly to embrace islands. In the north, you can see the southern end of large Szentendre Island, with a number of small hamlets on it. Next is a smaller one, once called Szunyog (Gnat) Island, with some shipyards. In the very heart of Budapest lies Margitsziget (Margaret Island), which is occupied by a beautiful park, hotels, restaurants, swimming pools and rowing and athletic clubs. At the southern extremity of Budapest stretches Csepelsziget (Csepel Island), almost 48 km. (30 miles) long, with extensive market gardens and a huge industrial complex, the Csepel Iron and Steel Works.

Standing on the top of Gellért Hill, you will see, south of the old fort and rising well above it, the 32-meter (110-ft.) high Liberation Memorial, commemorating the end of the 1944–45 siege and the Russian soldiers who fell in the seven-week battle. It is the work of Zsigmond Kisfaludy-Strobl, the famous Hungarian sculptor (1884–1975). Facing the Danube, you will have, on your left, two other hills—Várhegy (Castle Hill) and Rózsadomb (Hill of Roses). Beyond these, there is a range of higher hills, of which the conical Jánoshegy (John's Hill) is the tallest; its 529 meters (1,735 ft.) are topped by a lookout tower. Other Buda hills include the Széchenyi hegy and, further to the northwest, the Hármashatárhegy (Hill of Three Borders), both of which have their tourist centers, restaurants and hostels.

The Danube Bridges

Budapest had always been as proud of its bridges as London or Paris. Their total destruction by the retreating Nazi armies was as much of a blow as the wanton blowing-up of the Arno bridges at Florence. For many months, only a pontoon bridge connected the two halves of the city (Pest and Buda became one in 1873 when Óbuda, Old Buda, was also added to the capital), but all of the bridges were eventually rebuilt over the next 20 years. Farthest north is the railway bridge (reopened May 1955), which provides direct transport from the Hungarian coalfields into the heart of Budapest. Then follow the two bridges connecting Margaret Island with the city.

The Árpád Bridge was opened in 1950 and is the longest of all, two km. (over a mile) in length; it has recently been greatly widened. It connects the northern industrial suburbs of Újpest and Óbuda and is the only means of access by car to the beautiful island. The Margaret Bridge, at the southern tip, unusual in shape (it forms an obtuse angle in midstream, from which a short leg leads to the island), also had to be rebuilt, but its original design was retained. The bridge was blown up by the Nazis towards the end of 1944 when it was crowded with rush-hour traffic. Margaret Island contains, within a comparatively small space, the most attractive features of outdoor living in Budapest and lends the character of a holiday resort to the city during the summer. It is a park, sports center and spa and has two hotels.

The oldest of the Danube Bridges is the Lánchíd (Chain Bridge) designed in 1839 by the British engineer William Tierney Clark, who also designed London's Hammersmith Bridge, and finished ten years later by a compatriot, Adam Clark, who also built the 350-meter (383-yard) long tunnel under Castle Hill which connects the Danube Quay with the rest of Buda. The bridge was rebuilt and reopened in 1949, to mark the centenary of its inauguration.

South of the Chain Bridge, the Erzsébethíd (Elizabeth Bridge) is another graceful suspension bridge, in a single arch. It was the last of the bridges to be rebuilt and was reopened in 1964. Near its western end is a seated statue of Queen Elizabeth, the murdered wife of Franz Josef, who was greatly loved by the Hungarian people. She was crowned in the Matthias Church in 1867. The statue was badly damaged in the last war; it has now been restored and was recently re-erected on a new site, where the Queen sits close to the bridge named after her. Next is Szabadsághíd (Liberty Bridge), formerly named after Francis Joseph, which leads to the foot of Gellért Hill. Then comes the Petőfi Bridge, linking the Pest and Buda sides of the Grand Boulevard and finally a railway bridge.

Belváros, the Inner City

Modern Pest, much younger than Buda, has been conceived on a roughly concentric plan. The heart of Pest is the Belváros, or Inner City, which is enclosed by the Inner Boulevard, the first to be built. The second, or Grand Boulevard was built in the 1880s and 1890s and describes a semicircle from the Danube at Margaret Bridge in the north to Petőfi Bridge in the south. The third, outer, boulevard again forms a large semicircle around Pest, with the Danube as its diameter. The big boulevards are intersected by a number of straight main roads, such as Rákóczi Út, which radiate out from the center of the city and lead ultimately to the main national highways.

Sections of the Inner City have been converted into a pedestrian zone, which makes for peaceful sightseeing but neurotic driving. Parking can be a problem, and traffic crossing the area has to keep to two routes. There are parking lots at the edge of the zone, and indoor parking at designated points inside the zone.

Crossing the Danube from Buda by the Chain Bridge, you first reach the large oblong of Roosevelt Square. Here the statue of Count István Széchenyi, whom his most determined opponent,

Lajos Kossuth, dubbed "the greatest Hungarian," and the statue of Ferenc Deák, the architect of the Austro-Hungarian monarchy, stand close to one another; both men resided in this square. The large, neo-Renaissance building of the Academy of Sciences, on the left, forms a fitting background for Széchenyi, for it was he who donated a year's income to establish it in 1825.

On the far side of the square is the Gresham Building, an interesting art nouveau structure originally built for a British insurance company, and to the right stands the large new Atrium-Hyatt hotel.

Strolling southwards from Roosevelt Square, we find the so-called Korzó—a promenade reserved for pedestrians with many comfortable seats and several pleasant open-air cafes and restaurants—and a magnificent view. The first building on the Corso is the new Forum Hotel. Then follows Vigadó Square with, on the left, the Vigadó Concert Hall, built in a striking romantic style in the middle of the last century. Liszt, Brahms, Bartók and many other famous artists have given concerts here. It was gravely damaged during World War II, but is again one of the most important centers of Hungarian cultural life.

Soon there follows the Duna-Intercontinental Hotel, a massive modern building in which every bedroom overlooks the Danube. The Corso is a favorite strolling-place and the view of Buda and its historic palace and churches across the river affords a delightful panorama.

Walk down the Corso past the Intercontinental Hotel as far as Március 15 (March 15th) Square and turn left to penetrate the maze of narrow streets and closely-packed houses which lie behind it. This was the old walled city of medieval times; wherever the walls have been uncovered, they are preserved and marked with tablets. In this part of Pest are some of the oldest and finest churches. Two are in March 15th Square, forming a backdrop to the statue of Sándor Petőfi, the greatest 19th-century Hungarian poet. One is a Greek Orthodox church, built at the end of the 18th century, largely remodeled but still preserving some fine wood carvings and a late 18th-century iconostasis. The second is the Belvárosi plébánia templom (Inner City Parish Church), the oldest in Pest; its origins go back to the 12th century. There are hardly any architectural styles that cannot be traced in some part or other. The single nave still has its original Gothic chancel; two side chapels contain beautifully-carved Renaissance altar-pieces and tabernacles of red marble from the early 16th century. The 150 years of Turkish occupation are marked by a *mihrab,* a Muslim prayer niche. The organ of the Inner City Church was often played by Liszt who, between 1867 and 1875, lived only a few yards away. In his town house he regularly held "musical Sundays," at which Richard and Cosima Wagner were frequent guests.

To the east of the Corso, and parallel with it, is Váci Utca, which has Budapest's smartest shops. It is an excellent center for clothes, furs, shoes, books and folk art (the largest folk art shop is here); it is closed to motor traffic, as are several of its attractive side streets, and the whole area affords an agreeable area for window shopping, if no more. It has several popular small cafes, a new hotel, the Taverna, and the imposing International Trade Center. Just beyond Kigyó Utca (another popular shopping "mecca" and pedestrian precinct), Váci Utca crosses Szabadsajtó Út, a prolongation of Kossuth Lajos Utca, which is both a very busy traffic artery and the home of yet more fashionable stores. At the point where the roads cross lies Felszabadulás Tér (Liberation Square), with the headquarters of the Hungarian travel agency IBUSZ to the west and, to the east, an old Franciscan church. A bronze tablet on its wall shows a scene from the memorable flood of 1838, which devastated Pest and claimed many lives. The water rose over a meter (about four feet) above the pavement.

Beyond the Franciscan church, along Károlyi Mihály Utca (named after Count Michael Károlyi, who headed a short-lived democratic government at the end of World War I), we reach Kálvin Tér (Calvin Square), named after the Calvinist church whose classical facade dominates it. On the way we see on the right the University Church, one of the most beautiful Baroque buildings in the city. It was built between 1725 and 1742. Note especially the splendid Baroque pulpit. A short distance to the left is one of Budapest's most famous historic monuments, the National Museum. Built between 1837 and 1847, it is a fine example of 19th-century classicism, well proportioned and simple and surrounded by a large garden. Outside this famous building Sándor Petőfi recited his famous Nemzeti dal (National Song) on March 15 1848, calling the people to rise against the Habsburgs. There are two permanent exhibitions: (1) the prehistory of the people of Hungary (on the mezzanine floor; stone, bronze and iron ages plus Roman antiquities and collections of the Great Migrations); (2) history of the Hungarian people from the 9th to the 20th centuries.

Among the most precious and popular of the Museum's exhibits are the Hungarian royal regalia, including the Holy Crown of St. Stephen. These are impressively displayed in the "Hall of Honor." The crown, together with the scepter, the orb, the sword and the coronation robe were restored to Hungary in January 1978 by the United States, who had held them since 1945, when the fleeing Hungarian Army handed them over to prevent their falling into the hands of the Russians. The crown, a masterpiece of Byzantine art, is not now thought to be that presented by Pope Sylvester II in the year 1000 and with which Stephen was crowned first king of Hungary, but is believed to date from the 12th century. The regalia are regarded as the legal symbols of Hungarian sovereignty—even by a Communist government—as they provide evidence of unbroken statehood for close on a thousand years.

Rákóczi Út is the eastern continuation of Kossuth Lajos Utca and is the busiest shopping street of Pest, with several large department stores; it ends at the Keleti pályaudvar (East Station).

At the north end of Váci Utca is Vörösmarty Tér, with a statue of one of Hungary's great poets, Vörösmarty, and the famous Gerbeaud pastry shop, founded in 1857. Here the fashionable (and, nowadays, the not-so-fashionable) world meets for tea, coffee, or rich pastries. In and around this square are the chief airline offices, and not far away to the northeast is Engels Square, which contains the city's main long-distance bus terminal. Beyond this is the impressive St. Stephen's basilica, which was built in the second half of the 19th century; its 91-meter (300-ft.) high dome dominates the whole of Pest. Planned originally as a neo-Classical building, it was completed in neo-Renaissance style.

The district lying to the north of Vörösmarty Square is the Westminster and Whitehall of Budapest; most of the ministries are here, as well as the National Bank, the Courts of Justice and the Party Headquarters. Dominating the whole district, however, is the huge neo-Gothic Parliament building; its situation is particularly fine, as it is mirrored in the Danube in much the same way that the British Parliament is mirrored in the Thames. Its vast central dome, crowned by a red star, is well balanced by the arcades and the windows. It is now the center of Hungary's political life, with the offices of the Prime Minister and of the Presidential Council, which is elected by the National Assembly from among its members. The building is probably the city's most famous landmark.

The Grand Boulevard

The Grand Boulevard (Nagykörút) stretches from the two ends of the large loop which the Danube describes at Budapest, forming a wide semicircle. Laid out at the end of the 19th century, it shows the influence of Haussmann's Paris boulevards; an arm of the Danube was covered up, the bed of the river's backwater having been drained and banked, so that a broad thoroughfare, 35 meters (120 ft.) wide and almost five km. (three miles) long, could be created. The large apartment houses flanking much of its length were all built at about the same time and in the same architectural style.

Most of Budapest's theaters and many of its cinemas are situated on the Grand Boulevard and its sidestreets. Here, too, are several large cafes, a few nightclubs and a number of hotels. The Boulevard starts at the southern end, at Boráros Square; here it is called Ferenc Körút (Francis Boulevard), after the typical old district which it traverses. Then comes the section called József Körút (Joseph Boulevard). The main buildings of Lenin Körút (Lenin Boulevard), which follows, are the famous Hungária cafe-restaurant, the Hotel Royal and the Academy of Music. Lenin Körút ends at Marx Square, with the West Station. With a typical Hungarian sense of humor (or irony), the next section of the boulevard is named after St. Stephen (Szent István Körút); this ends at the Danube (Margaret Bridge). A stroll along the Grand Boulevard would take about an hour and a half and would be a good introduction to the busier parts of Budapest.

The grandest avenue of Budapest is the almost three-km. (two-mile) long Népköztársaság Útja (People's Republic Avenue). It was formerly known as Andrássy Ut, after the Hungarian statesman in whose time it was inaugurated, and has changed names several times since; at one time it was, inevitably, Stalin Avenue! It begins near the Basilica and finishes at Hősök Tere (Heroes' Square), at the entrance of the Városliget (City Park). It is lined with neo-Renaissance buildings, some of them with ornate but attractive facades. Under it runs Budapest's original underground (subway), the first on the European continent, which was opened in 1896. This, now known as Line 1, connects with the fine new Metro at Deák Tér, in the Inner City.

Not far from the Basilica stands the State Opera House, built between 1878 and 1884, in a neo-Renaissance style, by the architect Miklós Ybl. Badly damaged during the siege of 1944–45, it has been restored to its original splendor with the same loving care as was Vienna's Staatsoper; with the Ferenc Erkel Theater it is the center of Hungarian opera and ballet. The National Ballet School is conveniently housed just across the avenue in a large French Renaissance-style building known as the Drechsler Palace. This is the Shaftesbury Avenue or Broadway district of Budapest, in which half a dozen theaters are situated, including the Municipal Operetta Theater and the Vidám Színpad (Variety Stage).

The broad avenue continues after crossing Lenin Boulevard at November 7th Square. For the rest of its length it is bordered with trees and flower-beds.

Heroes' Square marks the end of Népköztársaság Útja—a spacious, attractively laid-out square that leads into the City Park. Here stand the impressive Millennial Monument commemorating the thousandth anniversary of the conquest of Hungary and the simple National War Memorial; it is here that every visiting foreign dignitary lays a wreath. On opposite sides of the square are two of the chief art galleries of Budapest—the Szépművészeti Múzeum (Museum of Fine Arts) and the Műcsarnok (Art Gallery), where all sorts of art exhibitions are held. The Szépművészeti is particularly rich in Flemish, Dutch and Spanish old masters—the latter perhaps the best collection outside Spain, including, as it does, seven fine El Grecos and five beautiful Goyas, as well as paintings by Velázquez and Murillo. The Italian School is represented by two superb paintings by Raphael, and others by Giorgione, Bellini, Correggio and Tintoretto. The Dutch and Flemish masters include three Rembrandts and works by Frans Hals, Rubens, Van Eyck, Memling, Van Dyck and Brueghel the Elder. Dürer and Cranach represent the German School, while the French have excellent pictures by Monet, Renoir, Gauguin and Cézanne. The British School is represented by Hogarth, Reynolds and Gainsborough. The sculpture collection aims to show the development of this art from the 4th to the 18th centuries; its "star item" is a small equestrian bronze statuette, attributed to Leonardo da Vinci. There is also a magnificent display of over 150,000 drawings, as well as an Egyptian and a Graeco-Roman exhibition.

The City Park

The City Park contains everything to delight children and adults alike. There is a big boating lake that becomes an artificial skating rink in winter, and a large fun fair, a circus and the Budapest zoo, as well as a rich botanical garden. Just south of the lake is a statue of George Washington; it was erected in 1906 from the donations of Hungarians who had emigrated to the United States. Here also is one of the most interesting museums in Hungary, the Mezőgazdasági Múzeum (Agricultural Museum). It is housed in a group of buildings representative of the national architecture throughout the centuries and has five sections: Hungarian and animal husbandry, forestry, horticulture, hunting and fishing and recent trophies.

The large Széchenyi Baths, built between 1909 and 1913, were extended in 1926 by open-air pools. They utilize some of the medicinal springs which have earned Budapest the title of "the Spa Capital."

South of the City Park, beyond the East Station, is the Népstadion (People's Stadium). It was opened in 1953 and can hold around 80,000 spectators. Nearby, close to the Népstadion Metro station, is the recently inaugurated Budapest Sportcsarnok or Sports Hall, which can seat over 12,000 and is used for sporting events, pop concerts and international congresses.

Óbuda

This section of the city—its name means "Old Buda"—is not without interest. Although its vast new apartment blocks are what first strike the eye, the heart of the suburb has been preserved in its entirety as an "ancient monument." In its center is the fine Baroque parish church and close by the beautiful Baroque former Zichy mansion, now a cultural center. While the site was being excavated, many interesting Roman remains were found, including an amphitheater; this could hold about 15,000 spectators. Óbuda is easily reached via the Árpád bridge, whose western bridgehead it forms, or by the electric railway from Batthyány Tér. Farther out, on the top of Hármashatárhegy (Hill of the Three Borders) there is a pleasant restaurant (*Hármashatárhegy* (M), tel. 888–780) which has a wide-ranging view over the city; it can be reached by bus.

The Buda Hills

These picturesque, thickly wooded hills rise to the west and northwest of the city and cover an area of some 16 by 19 km. (10 by 12 miles). They provide the "lungs" of Budapest as well as its largest playground—full of hikers and picnickers in the summer and skiers and tobogganists in the winter. They can easily be reached by public transport; a cogwheel railway starts opposite the Hotel Budapest and climbs to Széchenyi Hill. On Szilágyi Erzsébet Fasor, the wide, tree-lined avenue that leads to the Hotel Budapest, a statue has recently been erected to Count Raoul Wallenberg, the Swedish diplomat who saved the lives of about 100,000 Hungarian Jews during World War II and who was arrested, never to reappear, when the Red Army occupied Budapest. On Széchenyi Hill is the southern terminus of the Pioneers' Railway, a narrow-gauge line running for about 13 km. (eight miles) through the most attractive parts of the hills. With the exception of the engine-driver, all the jobs on the line are carried out by 12- to 14-year-old "Pioneers," the communist equivalent of scouts. A chairlift (*libegő*) runs from Zugligeti Road (bus 158 from Moszkva Tér) to Jánoshegy (John's Hill), the highest point of the hills. There are splendid views over Budapest from the hills, which offer endless opportunities for quiet, pleasant walks.

On the Dobogókő, a peak more than 700 meters (2,300 ft.) high, and lying some miles beyond the Buda Hills, is the Hotel Nimród, a favorite resort at weekends; it lies deep in thick forest. Another popular tourist objective is Ráckeve, on the island of Csepel, 48 km. (some 30 or so miles) south of Budapest. It has several picturesque buildings, including a Baroque mansion and a Serbian Orthodox church dating from 1487; a new resort complex, with motel, camping site and excellent opportunities for anglers, has recently been opened here.

PRACTICAL INFORMATION FOR BUDAPEST

TOURIST INFORMATION. *TOURINFORM* (Hungarian Tourist Board), Sütő Utca 2, in the Inner City, near the Deák Tér Metro station; open Mon. to Sat. 8–8, Sun. 8–1; tel. 179–800. The office answers all sorts of questions concerning tourism in Hungary in English, German, French and Russian. It also has a wide range of useful brochures.

IBUSZ Travel Bureau, Tanács Körút 3/c. *Budapest Tourist Board,* Roosevelt Tér 5. *Coopturist,* Kossuth Lajos Tér 13–15. *Volán Travel Bureau,* Október 6 Utca 11–13. *Express Youth and Students Travel Bureau,* Szabadság Tér 16. *Wagons-Lits/Cook,* Pilvax Köz 7. All these are in Pest, in or near the Inner City.

WHEN TO COME. At almost any time of the year, but avoid July and August if you don't like heat or crowds. During the winter, Budapest has a rich cultural program with many famous international artists. The International Fair is held in late May and mid-September; if you plan to visit Budapest then, book your hotel room well ahead. The theaters open in the fall and do not close until mid-June, while there are numerous art festivals in all but the two hottest summer months. The Budapest Spring Festival is a popular feature of March and the Budapest Musical Weeks of early fall. Sporting events are held throughout the year. Formula One motor racing and the Hungarian Grand Prix take place at Hungaroring, near Budapest, early in August.

GETTING AROUND BUDAPEST. By Tram and Trolley Bus. Fares are uniform on all trams and trolley buses. A yellow ticket, which must be bought in advance from tobacconists or special kiosks, entitles you to travel as far as you wish as long as you don't change lines. The fare is 2 Ft. The tickets must be self-canceled on the car; watch how the other passengers do it. Maps provided by the tourist offices tend to be insufficiently detailed, so arm yourself with one from one of the many bookshops in downtown Váci Utca or from any stationer's or card shop.

By Bus. The same regulations apply to buses as to trams and trolley buses, except that the fare is 3 Ft. and the ticket is blue. It is an offence to be caught with an uncanceled ticket and you could be fined 100 Ft. on the spot. This applies to trams and trolley buses and the subway as well.

By Subway. There is a highly efficient subway, or Metro; stations are marked with a capital M. The standard fare is 2 Ft. for any distance as long as you don't change lines. Line 2 runs from the eastern suburbs, past the East Station, through the Inner City area and under the Danube to the South Station. One of the stations, Moszkva Tér, is within easy walking distance of Castle Hill. Line 3 runs from the southern suburbs to Deák Square, in the Inner City, and northwards to the West Station and the northern suburbs. The same 2 Ft. yellow tickets are used as on trams; they are canceled at machines at the entrance; they are valid for one hour and should be kept until the end of the journey, as there are often checks by inspectors. The old subway, now line 1, unclearly marked "Földalatti", dates from 1896 (when it was the first on the European continent), but has been modernized; it runs from Vörösmarty Tér, in the heart of the Inner City, out to the City Park and beyond. It is useful to remember that all three lines meet at Deák Tér (Deák Square); see Budapest metro map.

There are local electric trains out to the suburbs (that to Szentendre starts from Batthyány Tér, on the Danube bank in Buda), an electric cogwheel railway, as well as a chair-lift, to the Buda Hills, and a funicular from the west end of the Chain Bridge up to Castle Hill.

A *napijegy* (day ticket), costing 24 Ft., allows unlimited travel for a day on all municipal transport within the city boundaries.

By Taxi. You will find taxis outside hotels, rail stations, theaters and at the main street corners, or they may be hailed while cruising. When free, they display the illuminated sign "TAXI." You can order them by telephone, dialing 222–222 or 666–666. There are also a number of private taxis (which will have the name and address of the owner on the side of

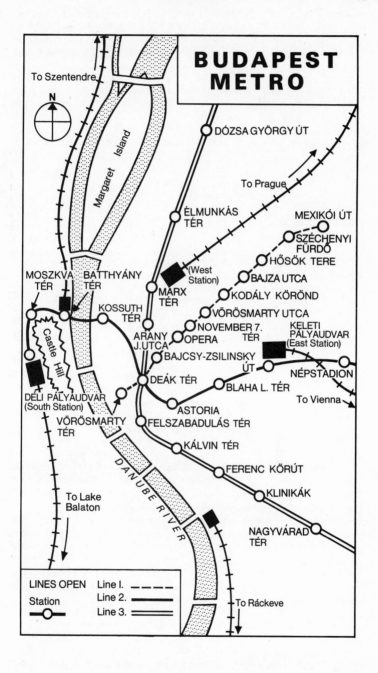

BUDAPEST METRO

To Szentendre

N

Margaret Island

DÓZSA GYÖRGY ÚT

To Prague

ÉLMUNKÁS TÉR

MEXIKÓI ÚT

SZÉCHENYI FÜRDŐ

HŐSÖK TERE

MOSZKVA TÉR

BATTHYÁNY TÉR

(West Station)

BAJZA UTCA

KODÁLY KÖRÖND

MARX TÉR

VÖRÖSMARTY UTCA

KOSSUTH TÉR

NOVEMBER 7. TÉR

KELETI PÁLYAUDVAR (East Station)

Castle Hill

ARANY J.UTCA

OPERA

BAJCSY-ZSILINSKY ÚT

NÉPSTADION

DEÁK TÉR

BLAHA L. TÉR

DÉLI PÁLYAUDVAR (South Station)

To Vienna

VÖRÖSMARTY TÉR

ASTORIA

FELSZABADULÁS TÉR

KÁLVIN TÉR

D A N U B E   R I V E R

FERENC KÖRÚT

KLINIKÁK

To Lake Balaton

NAGYVÁRAD TÉR

LINES OPEN

Station

Line I. – – – –
Line 2. ▬▬▬▬
Line 3. ════

To Ráckeve

the cab). The hiring charge is 10 Ft., plus 8 Ft. per km. and 3 Ft. per minute waiting charge. Private taxis (many of which have no meters) charge the same in theory, but one can come across a greedy driver from time to time.

By Boat. In summer, a regular service of boats links the north and south of the city, calling at points on both banks (including Margaret Island). In addition, and also only during the summer, there are special pleasure trips by boat, leaving the pier at Vigadó Tér, in the Inner City; they run each afternoon and evening and also on Sunday morning. The trips last from up to two hours; there is a restaurant, cafe and dance band on board.

Car Hire. This can most easily be arranged through the travel desk of your hotel. Avis, Hertz and other firms operate in Budapest; there is an Avis desk at the airport. Rates are from $15 a day up, plus from 15 cents a mile, or from $216 a week with unlimited mileage. A refundable deposit of $150 must be paid.

HOTELS. In spite of an ambitious building program, there can still be a shortage of rooms during the tourist season (May to September) and it is absolutely essential to book accommodations well in advance. Even in spring and fall, all but the best hotels tend to be overcrowded. In addition, Budapest is becoming increasingly popular as the venue of international congresses and conferences, during which hundreds of rooms are preempted. Single rooms with bath are scarce except in the best hotels. At almost any time of the year the lower grades of hotels tend to be overcrowded with package tour groups and individual travelers wishing for a high standard of service are therefore recommended to use hotels of a higher category.

If you arrive in Budapest without a reservation, go to the IBUSZ office at Petőfi Tér 3, just behind the Intercontinental Hotel, or, for travelers arriving by air, the tourist office at Ferihegy Airport.

Deluxe

Atrium-Hyatt, Roosevelt Tér 2, Budapest V. (tel. 383–000). Large luxury hotel, opened in 1982, in the Inner City with fine view over the Danube. 356 air-conditioned rooms, all with bath and color television. Several restaurants, cocktail bar, covered swimming pool, sauna and gym. Ballroom; conference rooms with every facility for businessmen.

Duna-Intercontinental, Apáczai Csere János Utca 4, Budapest V. (tel. 175–122). On the Danube Quay in the Inner City; its 340 rooms and suites, all with bath, overlook the Danube. Several restaurants, cafe with terrace overlooking the river, penthouse bar and nightclub; swimming pool and squash court. Fully-equipped conference rooms. Garage. Air-conditioned throughout.

Hilton, Hess András Tér 1–3, Budapest I. (tel. 751–000). In a magnificent position on Castle Hill, with a splendid view over the city. The hotel incorporates the tower and other remains of a 13th-century church. 323 rooms and suites, all with bath. Several restaurants, nightclub, fully-equipped conference rooms. Garage. Full air-conditioning. The Casino, a joint Hungarian-Austrian venture, only accepts hard currency; roulette, baccara and blackjack are played. Winnings are tax-free and may be exported.

BUDAPEST 83

Thermal, Margitsziget, Budapest XIII. (tel. 321–100). This luxurious hotel on Margaret Island has 206 rooms, all with private bath and other amenities; thermal swimming pool and medicinal baths. Medical supervision of any treatment desired. Sauna, gym. Excellent restaurant, in which kosher food can be supplied to order; conference hall and nightclub (*Havanna*); pleasant outdoor cafe. Direct bus to Marx Tér, north of the city center.

Expensive

Béke, Lenin Körút 97, Budapest VI. (tel. 323–300). Traditional hotel near the West Station, completely modernized and refurbished with air-conditioning throughout, 246 rooms, all with TV and mini-bar. Several restaurants, bars, and famous *Orfeum* nightclub. Garage.

Buda-Penta, Krisztina Körút 41–43, Budapest I. (tel. 566–333). New hotel in Buda, near South Station and Metro terminal. 399 rooms with bath, TV and mini-bar. Public rooms air-conditioned. Restaurants, cafe, nightclub, indoor swimming pool, sauna, gym; garage.

Budapest, Szilágyi Erzsébet Fasor 53–55, Budapest II. (tel. 153–230). 280 double rooms, all with bath. Restaurant, wine bar, cafe and rooftop bar with spectacular view and dancing. A striking circular building in a pleasant part of Buda, opposite the lower terminus of the cog-wheel railway to the Buda Hills.

Flamenco, Tas Vezér Utca 7, Budapest XI. (tel. 252–250). 336 rooms with bath, TV and mini-bar. New hotel in the Buda green belt, run by Spanish interests; restaurant and bar feature Spanish specialties. Public rooms air-conditioned. Swimming pool, sauna, indoor tennis court. Garage.

Forum, Apáczai Csere János Utca 12–14, Budapest V. (tel. 178–0880). On Danube bank in the Inner City. 408 rooms with bath, TV and mini-bar. Several restaurants, bar, swimming pool, sauna, gym. Conference halls and ballrooms. Underground garage. This has been chosen by American Express as the best of the 80 world-wide Forum hotels. The hotel is air-conditioned throughout.

Gellért, Szent Gellért Tér 1, Budapest XI. (tel. 852–200). 235 rooms with bath or shower. Partial air-conditioning. Thermal swimming pools and baths. Outdoor terrace restaurant overlooking Danube. Splendidly traditional and warmly recommended.

Grand Hotel Margitsziget, Margitsziget, Budapest XIII. (tel. 321–100). Completely rebuilt historic hotel on Margaret Island; guests may use the spa facilities of the Hotel Thermal, to which it is connected by an underground passage. 174 rooms, all with bath, balcony, color TV and mini-bar.

Hungária, Rákóczi Út 90, Budapest VII. (tel. 229–050). 528 rooms, all doubles and most singles with bath or shower; all rooms have color TV and mini-bar. This completely reconstructed and refurbished hotel is also Budapest's largest. Situated opposite the East Station, with a Metro station nearby, it is triple-glazed against noise and has several bars, restaurants and a nightclub. Also has sauna, gym, and underground garage. Dogs are welcome.

Novotel, Alkotás Utca 63–67, Budapest XII. (tel. 869–588). New hotel on main road into city from the west. 324 rooms with fine views, all with bath and TV. Public rooms air-conditioned. Swimming pool, sauna, tennis courts, restaurants and bar. Large new Congress-hall complex.

Taverna, Váci Utca 20, Budapest V. (tel. 384–999). New hotel in the Inner City, close to the International Trade Center. 224 rooms, all with bath or shower, radio and mini-bar. Restaurant, beer hall and grill room; sauna.

Moderate

Astoria, Kossuth Lajos Utca 19, Budapest V. (tel. 173–411). Traditional hotel at busy Inner City crossroads; recently modernized and sound-proofed. Most rooms with bath or shower. Good restaurant, cafe, night-club, sauna, gym.

Emke, Akácfa Utca 3–5, Budapest VII. (tel. 229–230). Centrally located just off busy Rákóczi Út. 70 doubles with bath. Restaurant, cafe and noted nightclub (*Maxim's*).

Erzsébet, Károlyi Mihály Utca 11–15, Budapest V. (tel. 382–111). Well-known old hotel in the Inner City, completely modernized and refurbished. 123 rooms, mostly doubles, all with shower, TV and mini-bar. Public rooms air-conditioned. Restaurant and popular beer hall (*János Pince*).

Európa, Hárshegyi Utca 5–7, Budapest II. (tel. 767–122). This 13-story hotel is situated high above Buda, with fine views, and is surrounded by woods. 20 single and 138 double rooms, all with bath. Restaurant, bar.

Olympia, Eötvös Út 40, Budapest XII. (tel. 568–011). Situated in the Buda Hills, with easy access to town. 172 rooms, most with bath. Restaurant, conference room, bars, nightclub with floorshow; swimming pool, sauna, gym. A few minutes' walk will take you into the Buda woods.

Palace, Rákóczi Út 43, Budapest VIII. (tel. 136–000). 93 rooms, some doubles with bath. Good restaurant, bar and nightclub. In the main shopping street.

Royal, Lenin Körút, Budapest VII. (tel. 533–133). Large hotel in central, but somewhat noisy, situation in the heart of the theater district. Recently refurbished. 360 rooms, all with bath. Restaurant, cafe, bar, nightclub, gym.

Vörös Csillag, Rege Út 21, Budapest XII. (tel. 750–522). Built in hunting-lodge style 1,000 feet above the Danube and close to the upper terminus of the cog-wheel railway. Both single and double rooms with bath. Restaurants, bar, open-air terrace with splendid view. Swimming pool, sauna. In the adjoining wooded grounds are 54 self-catering bungalows; occupants have the use of all the hotel's facilities.

Inexpensive

Citadella, Gellért Hegy, Budapest XI. (tel. 665–794). In the former fortress, with fine view over the city. Recently completely refurbished, this is primarily suitable for young people; its rooms have two to four beds each and all have hot and cold running water; there are showers in the corridors. Very popular restaurant, beer hall and nightclub.

Expo, Dobi István Utca 10, Budapest X. (tel. 842–130). Adjoining the Trade Fair grounds and some way from the city center, this hotel is intended chiefly for businessmen, for whom it has every facility. 160 rooms with bath, radio and mini-bar. Restaurant, conference rooms.

Metropol, Rákóczi Út 58, Budapest VII. (tel. 421–175). Rather old-fashioned hotel on main shopping street, but recommended for comfort and courtesy. 102 rooms; there are both singles and doubles with bath. Restaurant, cafe.

Stadion, Ifjúság Utca 1–3, Budapest XIV. (tel. 631–830). Large hotel in eastern part of city, near sports stadium and Metro station. 379 rooms with bath or shower. Restaurant, swimming pool, sauna.

Volga, Dózsa György Utca 65, Budapest XIII. (tel. 290–200). North of city center, but with direct Metro connection. 308 rooms with bath or shower, all with two or more beds. Restaurants, bars, amusement arcade. Very popular with groups.

Wien, Budaörsi Út 88, Budapest XI. (tel. 665–4000). In southwestern outskirts, near junction of Vienna and Lake Balaton motorways. 110 double rooms, many with bath. Restaurant, cafe, petrol station and repair shop.

MOTEL. Vénusz, Dósa Utca 2–4, Budapest III. (tel. 687–252). Near Danube bank north of city; 76 doubles and 3 suites, all with bath. Restaurant, cafe, water sports, tennis.

GUEST HOUSES (Pensions). There are now a good many small, privately-owned guest houses in Budapest and in the principal tourist resorts. They usually have twin-bedded rooms and adequate bath and toilet facilities, with hot and cold running water; a few have rooms with private bath. A "family" atmosphere prevails. Not all have restaurants, though there is always one close by. For details, apply to TOURINFORM, Sütő Útca 2, Budapest V (in the Inner City, near the Deák Tér Metro station).

TOURIST HOSTELS. There are several of these in and around Budapest, suited above all to young people. The **Strand,** Pusztakúti Utca 3, Budapest III, lies some miles north of the city but is easily reached by electric suburban railway from Batthány Tér; mainly dormitory accommodations. There is a restaurant close by.

Arrangements for these hostels are best made through IBUSZ. The Express Travel Bureau (Szabadság Tér 16, near the American Embassy) can arrange accommodations for young people in university hostels during July and August only.

CAMPING. "Holiday Village," at **Hárshegy,** in the Buda woods. There are 35 bungalows, 70 log cabins and space for 500 campers. There is also a campsite at **Római Fürdő,** near the Danube, north of the city (open-air baths), with room for 1,500 campers, who may use the adjacent Vénusz motel restaurant. Details from Budapest Tourist, Roosevelt Tér 5 (opposite the eastern end of the Chain Bridge), or from the Hungarian Camping and Caravanning Club, Üllői Út 6, Budapest VIII.

PRIVATE HOUSES. IBUSZ (at its office at Petőfi Tér 3, behind the Duna-Intercontinental Hotel), as well as the other main tourist offices, can make arrangements for you to stay in private houses. You will be provided with a clean, comfortable bedroom, with use of the bathroom facilities, but with no service. Some of the houses have cooking facilities, but breakfast is not normally provided.

RESTAURANTS. Prices in Budapest restaurants vary quite considerably depending on whether or not an orchestra is playing, so that, for instance, a portion of goose that costs 200 Ft. at lunch may cost 250 Ft. or more at dinner. However, a good meal, with half a bottle of wine, can be had for between 350 and 500 Ft. a head and in some of the smaller places (where the food may be even better) for half that sum. A *menü* (fixed-price menu) of two or three courses can be had at many restaurants for as little as 60 Ft.

Nearly all restaurants are state-owned but a few, generally small ones, are offered on lease to the highest bidder and are granted licenses to sell food and drink at controlled prices.

Our grading of the restaurants, inns and taverns of Budapest that we list is based not on their official classification, but on reasonable standards of cuisine, comfort, atmosphere and value for money. At the more fashionable places it is generally necessary to book a table; check with your hotel porter. We have divided the restaurants, other than those at the hotels, into three categories: Expensive (E), Moderate (M) and Inexpensive (I), though there are, inevitably, borderline cases. Furthermore, we have separated them into those on the west bank of the Danube (Buda) and those on the east bank (Pest).

A large proportion of Hungarian restaurants have some kind of music, though only in the evening. This can range from a soft lute or piano to a full gypsy orchestra. The music is, of course, part of the Hungarian "scene" and diners will sit near to, or away from, the music according to their tastes.

The better hotels (the 5-star and 4-star establishments) all have excellent restaurants. The more luxurious of them have several each, one, in most cases, serving international food and another specializing in Hungarian dishes. The better restaurants and those in the more expensive hotels expect their male guests to wear a tie in the evening. It is important to realize that nearly all restaurants, though not those in the hotels, are closed one day a week; make enquiries of your hotel porter, who will also reserve a table for you. We have listed first the restaurants in Buda, then those in Pest.

Buda

Expensive

Alabárdos, Országház Utca 12 (tel. 160–828). On Castle Hill; small, intimate restaurant in a beautiful building with period decor. Outstanding food, wine and service, with soft music. Open evenings only; booking and suitable dress essential.

Arany Hordó, Tárnok Utca 16 (tel. 566–765). Historic 14th-century building on Castle Hill. Its specialty is the *fogas,* the delicious fish from Lake Balaton. Dining room, beer hall and wine cellar. Open from noon; gypsy music in the evenings.

Fortuna, Hess András Tér 4 (tel. 756–857). In an ancient palace in the heart of the Castle district. Very good food, a distinguished wine list and, in the evenings, a gypsy orchestra. Open from noon. Booking is recommended, even for lunch.

Régi Országház, Országház Utca 17 (tel. 750–650). A very old, rebuilt, inn at the northern end of Castle Hill. Seven rooms, each decorated in a different style. Famous for its wines. Open all day; gypsy music in the evenings.

Rózsadomb, Bimbó Út 2 (tel. 353–847). Excellent restaurant, beer hall and (cheaper) snack bar between Castle Hill and the Margaret Bridge. Warmly praised by Western visitors.

Moderate

Fehér Galamb, Szent Háromság Utca 9 (tel. 756–975). Attractive restaurant a few yards from the Matthias Church, in the Castle district. Open from mid-afternoon. Its specialty is meat roasted on the spit. Gypsy music. Book.

Kacsa, Fö Utca 75 (tel. 353–357). Small elegant restaurant near the Buda river bank. Excellent wines and duck specialties. Highly recommended for late diners. Open till 2 A.M.

Kisbuda, Frankel L. Utca 34 (tel. 152–244). Near the Buda end of the Margaret Bridge with an attractive garden terrace in summer. Recommended for generous portions of fish and meat specialties. A piano and violin duo play in the evenings. Closed on Sunday evenings.

Margitkert, Margit Utca 15 (tel. 354–791). Not far from the western end of the Margaret Bridge. Smart and very popular with both locals and foreign visitors, this typical Buda restaurant, established in 1776, holds the Golden Plaque of the International Association of Gastronomic Writers. Open from noon; gypsy music in the evenings. Must book.

Tabáni Kakas, Attila Út 27 (tel. 757–165). A delightful small restaurant to the west of Castle Hill. Specializes in poultry dishes and is famous for its goose. Pianist plays and sings.

Vadrózsa, Pentelei Molnár Utca 15 (tel. 351–118). In the garden of a private villa. The food, and especially the goose liver (not cheap), is highly praised. Open evenings only during the week, also for lunch on Sundays.

Inexpensive

Halászkert, Lajos Utca 46 (tel. 686–480). Very popular old Buda (Ó Buda) fish restaurant with long tables and lively gypsy music in the evenings. Fiery fish soup is a specialty.

Hídvendéglő, Mókus Utca 22 (tel. 886–938). Typical small old Buda restaurant, with accordion music. Open evenings only.

Márvány Menyasszony, Márvány Utca 6 (tel. 756–165). Charming garden restaurant not far from the South Station. Rooms decorated in Hungarian peasant style. Open all day; music and dancing in the evenings.

Náncsi Néni, Ördögárok Utca 80 (tel. 167–830). A small, often crowded, family restaurant with good food; some way out. Closed on Wednesdays; open all day on other weekdays and till 5 P.M. on Sundays.

Pest-Buda, Fortuna Utca 3 (tel. 569–849). Charmingly decorated little restaurant on Castle Hill, with good food and very friendly service. Towards the top of the (I) range. Open lunch and dinner; old-time music in the evenings.

Szeged, Bartók Béla Út 1 (tel. 251–268). A short distance from the Danube, near the west end of the Szabadság (Liberty) Bridge. Traditional restaurant, specializing in fish dishes. Gypsy music in the evening.

Pest

Expensive

Gundel, Állatkerti Út 2 (tel. 221–002). In the City Park. Famous old restaurant; excellent food and wine; outdoor tables. Gypsy music in the evenings. It has an (M) section, named the "Bagolyvár".

Hanna, Dob Utca 35 (tel. 427–359). This is a much frequented kosher restaurant, not far from the Jewish Synagogue and Museum. It is run in conjunction with the Orthodox Jewish community and also supplies kosher food to the Hotel Thermal.

Hungária, Lenin Körút 9 (tel. 223–849). Famous cafe-restaurant, opened in 1894, when it was known as the *New York.* Destroyed in World War II, it has been rebuilt and redecorated in all its original art nouveau splendor. Open for lunch and dinner; in the evening music and dancing. The food and service are variously judged.

Kárpátia, Károlyi Mihály Utca 4 (tel. 170–303). In the heart of the Inner City. Very good food; pleasant outdoor terrace and garden. Gypsy music in the evenings. Low-calorie menus for those on a diet.

Légrádi Testvérek, Magyar Utca 23 (tel. 186–804). Intimate and charminglyfurnished restaurant in the Inner City, with excellent food. Open Monday through Friday, evenings only. Warmly recommended.

Százéves, Pesti Barnabás Utca 2 (tel. 183–608). Just off Váci Utca, in the Inner City. Good food and wine in an 18th-century Baroque palace. Charming old-fashioned booths for private eating. In the evening the gypsy music can sometimes be a bit overpowering for so intimate a place. Unless you order carefully, the check may come as a nasty shock.

Moderate

Apostolok, Kigyó Utca 4–6 (tel. 183–704). Famous beer hall and restaurant in the Inner City pedestrian precinct. Good hot food all day and tasty cold dishes in the evenings. Excellent beer.

Dunakorzó, Vigadó Tér 3 (tel. 186–435). In a delightful position right on the Corso, overlooking the Danube and Buda. Outdoor terrace. Good and reasonably-priced food. Open all day; music in the evening.

Kispipa, Akácfa Utca 38 (tel. 422–587). Very popular restaurant in the heart of Pest. Open all day; piano music in the evenings.

Mátyáspince, Március 15. Tér 8 (tel. 181–693). Famous restaurant in the Inner City, close to the Elizabeth Bridge. Upper limit of the (M) range. Both food and service are excellent and it is always full for lunch. One of Hungary's best-known gypsy bands plays in the evenings. Book your table.

Múzeum, Múzeum Körút 12 (tel. 138–282). Recently refurbished, very popular restaurant next to the National Museum. Frequented by staff of the neighboring University. No music. Open all day.

Opera, Népköztársaság Útja 44 (tel. 328–586). Recently refurbished restaurant and beer hall in the heart of the theater district, with outdoor tables. Italian food specialties. Gypsy music in the evening. Popular for a meal after the show.

Vigadó, Vigadó Tér (tel. 176–222). Beer hall with excellent food in elegant surroundings. It is in the newly rebuilt Vigadó Concert Hall, in the Inner City.

Inexpensive

Alföldi, Kecskeméti Utca 4 (tel. 174–404). In the Inner City not far from Kálvin Tér (Calvin Square). Typically Hungarian, with very good food, and much-frequented by university students. Outdoor terrace in summer.

Bástya, Rákóczi Út 29 (tel. 139–409). Very popular and often crowded restaurant in the city's main shopping thoroughfare. Quick and friendly service. Open all day. No music.

Csárnok, Rosenberg hp. 11 (tel. 312–951). Small, lively restaurant near the U.S. Embassy. Serves Hungarian draught beer and excellent food. No music. Closed on weekends.

Kiskakukk, Pozsonyi Út 12 (tel. 321–732). Near Pest end of Margaret Bridge. Good, simple food and willing service.

Lucullus, Lenin Körút 7 (tel. 223–001). Despite its name, extremely simple, but with good, honest Hungarian food and attentive service. On Grand Boulevard, near Rákóczi Út; no music.

Rézkakas, Veres Pálné Utca 3 (tel. 180–038). In the Inner City, just south of the pedestrian precinct. Simply furnished, but with good food; poultry a specialty. No music.

FOREIGN-STYLE RESTAURANTS. There are a good many of these, most of them in the Moderate (M) or Inexpensive (I) categories. Here is a selection:

Bajkál (Russian), at the corner of Kossuth Lajos Utca and Semmelweis Utca, in the Inner City (tel. 176–839). Excellent tea; open all day.

Bukarest (Romanian), Bartók Béla Út 48, beyond the Hotel Gellért, in Buda (tel. 252–203). Open all day; dancing in the evening.

Étoile (French), Pozsonyi Ut 4. Near Pest end of Margaret Bridge (tel. 122–242). Accordion music in the evening; dancing.

Görög Taverna (Greek), Csengeri Utca (tel. 410–722). Delightful Mediterranean-style restaurant serving Greek and Hungarian food and wine. Open every day.

Havanna (Latin-American), Bajcsy-Zsilinszky Út 21 (tel. 121–039). Open all day; Latin-American music in the evenings.

Karczma Polska-Kis Royal (Polish), Márvány Utca, near the South Station (tel. 151–069). Beer hall open all day, restaurant in the evening only.

Prágai Svejk (Czech), Kürt Utca 16 (tel. 223–023); Czech food and Czech beer.

Szechuan (Chinese), Roosevelt Tér 5 (tel. 172–407). At Pest end of Chain Bridge. This (E) restaurant is furnished in Chinese style. Soft Chinese music in the evenings. Book well ahead.

Szerb (Serbian), Nagy Ignac Utca 16 (tel. 111–858). Near the Pest end of Margaret Bridge. Friendly and always busy. Serves two-pint glasses of beer.

Szófia (Bulgarian), Kossuth Lajos Tér 13–15, behind the Parliament (tel. 118–232).

BEER AND WINE RESTAURANTS. Most of the larger hotels have both a wine cellar (*borozó*) and a beer cellar (*söröző*), so we do not list these separately. We must, however, mention the *Borkatakomba* (Wine Catacombs) at Budafok, a southwestern suburb of Budapest. Here there is a whole series of vaults cut into the limestone. The caves are decorated in Hungarian style and a gypsy band plays Hungarian folksongs. Excellent simple Hungarian food; open in the evening only.

In the center of the Inner City, just behind the Hotel Intercontinental, is the *Rondella,* Régi Posta Utca 4, a wine cellar which is also an inexpensive restaurant—though the accent is on the wine, not the food. There are wine bars and beer halls in most of the streets of the Inner City; they are to be found, too, all over Budapest.

SNACK BARS. *Bisztró* or *ételbár* are to be found in almost every street in the busier parts of the city. Those most conveniently situated and most

likely to be of use to the visitor include: *Mézes Mackó,* Kigyó Utca, in
the Inner City pedestrian precinct; *Savoy* and *Abbazia,* Népköztársaság
Útja 48 and 49, opposite each other where the avenue crosses the Grand
Boulevard; and *Casino,* on Margaret Island. A bright new McDonald's
has just opened off Váci Utca.

There are many self-service restaurants *(önkiszolgáló étterem);* these,
however, may present difficulties if you do not speak Hungarian, or recog-
nize Hungarian dishes.

PASTRY SHOPS AND CAFES. Among the most popular pastry shops
are the fashionable and crowded *Gerbeaud,* in Vörösmarty Tér, in the
heart of the Inner City; the *Korona,* in Dísz Tér, near the Castle; the *Rusz-
wurm,* near the Matthias Church (open since 1827); the *Angelika,* in Batthyány Tér, on the west bank of the Danube, frequented by the literary
and artistic world; the *Különlegességi,* at Népköztársaság Útja 70 and the
Hauer, at Rákóczi Út 49. The *Hungária,* already mentioned as a well-
known restaurant, also has a much-frequented pastry shop and cafe. The
Bécsi Kávéház in the Forum Hotel is reputed to have the best cream cakes
in town.

There are innumerable small coffee bars (in Hungarian *eszpresszó*).
Three of these, very conveniently situated for shoppers, are in the Inner
City pedestrian precinct; they are the *Anna,* at Váci Utca 7 (which turns
into a popular night spot when the shops close), the *Muskátli,* at Váci Utca
11 (which serves good tea) and the *Nárcisz,* Váci Utca 32, on the corner
of Kigyó Utca. All have terraces on the street, where one can see—and
be seen.

MUSEUMS. The many museums and picture galleries of Budapest offer
a wide choice of interesting works of art and other exhibits. They have
been considerably enriched by the fact that the People's Republic has nationalized all great private collections, though several smaller collections
remain in private hands. For a country that has been looted so frequently
in the course of centuries, Hungary has managed to retain a remarkable
quantity of artistic and historical treasures. Museum visiting hours are
normally from 10 A.M. to 6 P.M. except on Mondays, when museums are
closed. The entrance fee is usually 5–20 Ft. with admission normally free
on Saturdays. Check details with your hotel porter or a tourist office.

Bélyegmúzeum (Stamp Museum), Hársfa Utca 37. Contains all Hungarian stamps ever issued. Open Sun., Wed., Sat. (Metro: Blaha Lujza
Tér.)

Budapesti Történeti Múzeum (Budapest History Museum), in block E
of the former Royal Palace. Medieval history and art of Buda fortress and
the capital city.

Hadtörténeti Múzeum (War History Museum), Tóth Árpád Sétány 40,
Budapest I. Contains rich collections of Turkish and Napoleonic periods,
plus documents of Hungarian military history. Open 9–5 daily.

Iparművészeti Múzeum (Museum of Applied and Decorative Arts),
Üllői Út 33–37, near the southern end of the Grand Boulevard. This is
a building in modern Hungarian style. There are two permanent exhibitions: the history of ceramic art from Grecian vases to china from the great
contemporary porcelain workshops; and the goldsmith's art in Europe
from the 16th to the 20th centuries. (Metro: Ferenc Körút.)

Közlekedési Múzeum (Transport Museum), in the Városliget (City Park). Covers the field of transport in Hungary. Closed Fri. (Metro: Széchenyi Fürdő.)

Mezőgazdasági Múzeum (Agricultural Museum), in the City Park, is housed in buildings representing the national architecture throughout the centuries. Open 9–5 daily. (Metro: Hősök Tere.)

Nagytétényi Kastély Múzeum (Nagytétény Castle Museum), Csókási Pál Útca 9; the museum, which is in a southwestern suburb, has an interesting collection of Hungarian and foreign furniture and is itself a beautiful Baroque castle.

Nemzeti Galéria (National Gallery), in the central blocks (B, C, and D) of the former Royal Palace on Castle Hill. It contains a representative display of Hungarian fine art throughout the ages. Open Tues. 12–6, Wed. 12–8, Thurs. to Sun. 10–6.

Nemzeti Múzeum (National Museum), Múzeum Körút 14–16, Budapest VIII. A mid-19th-century building in neo-Classical style with two permanent exhibitions displaying the prehistory and history of the Hungarian people in addition to the very popular royal regalia. (Metro: Kálvin Tér.)

Néprajzi Múzeum (Ethnographical Museum), Kossuth Lajos Tér 12, Budapest V. A branch of the National Museum, this contains Hungarian folk art and folklore collections. A collection of the art of Oceania is also housed here. Library. (Metro: Kossuth Tér.)

Szépművészeti Múzeum (Fine Arts Museum), Dózsa György Út 41, at the end of Népköztásaság Út ja, at the edge of the City Park. This contains the largest collection of paintings and sculpture in Hungary. Not all rooms are open at the same time. (Metro: Hősök Tere.)

Zsidó Gyűjtemény (Jewish Museum), Dohany Útca 2. History of the Hungarian Jews; religious relics and works of art. Open Apr. 15 to Oct. 31, on Mon. and Thurs. 2–6, Tues., Wed., Fri. and Sun. 10–1. Closed Sat. and Jewish hols. (Metro: Deák Tér.)

OPERA, CONCERTS, THEATER. For details of all events consult the monthly *Programme* which is available free at your hotel. Tickets can be obtained from the Budapest Tourist Board, Roosevelt Tér 5, Budapest V, from the Booking Office at 1, Vörösmarty Square, or from the Central Booking Agency for the Theaters, Népköztársaság Útja 18, Budapest VI. Even simpler, you can ask the information desk of your hotel to get them for you. Prices are comparatively low. It is also sometimes possible to obtain a ticket at the box office on the day of performance.

The Lido, Felszabadulás Tér, in the heart of the Inner City, provides food and entertainment all day. Its attractions include a folklore show in the afternoon, followed by jazz music. In the evening an all-woman band plays during dinner, after which there is a variety show. Gambling-machines (for forints) will attract some.

Opera and theater. There are two opera houses in Budapest, under the same management—the *State Opera House* (on Népköztársaság Útja 22), recently restored to its original splendor, and the *Erkel Theater,* Köztársaság Tér 30, near the East Station. Dress is almost always informal, even on gala occasions.

There are some 20 permanent theaters in Budapest and in summer performances are given on open-air stages. Performances usually begin at 7 P.M. at open-air theaters (in the summer at 8 P.M.).

Concerts. There is a year-round feast for music-lovers in Budapest. Apart from the Opera and the Erkel Theater, musical life is centered on the *Academy of Music* (Liszt Ferenc Tér 8, near Népköztársaság Útja), which has a large and a small concert hall, and the newly reopened *Vigadó,* on the Danube quay.

Hungary has an inexhaustible fund of chamber orchestras. The Tátrai String Quartet and the Budapest Wind Quintet, the Bartók String Quartet, the Kodály String Quartet and the Ferenc Liszt Chamber Orchestra all give regular performances throughout the country and abroad. The Hungarian Chamber Orchestra has a changing number of members, but no conductor.

The Hungarian State Concert Orchestra gives the greatest number of concerts in Budapest, The Symphony Orchestra of the Hungarian Radio and Television has also given a growing number of performances since the early Sixties. Finally, the Philharmonic Orchestra (about 110 years old) of the State Opera House sometimes finds additional time to give concerts.

Choral singing is an old tradition in Hungary, which has been greatly developed by Zoltán Kodály's pioneering work in musical education. Handel's and Bach's oratorios and cantatas are performed annually; many baroque concertos and orchestral compositions are frequently presented.

The Budapest Spring Festival of Music is usually held in March; the Budapest Musical Weeks are one of the attractions of early fall. They have featured competitions for pianists, for singers, for cellists and for chamber music. In the fall of 1962, a Jazz Club was founded for young people in Budapest, which meets weekly; it has more than a thousand members. Excellent church music can be heard at the Matthias or Coronation Church on Castle Hill. Not only are concerts and organ recitals given here, but the High Mass on Sundays at 10 A.M. is sung by a large and well-trained choir, to the accompaniment of an orchestra. There is also good church music at the Basilica and at the Inner City Parish Church, on the Pest side of the Elizabeth Bridge. Around Easter, concerts of oratorios are performed at the Lutheran church in Deák Tér.

Cinema. In addition to Hungarian films, some of which are outstandingly good, cinemas usually show half a dozen foreign films in the original language each week.

NIGHTLIFE. Unlike most other Eastern European capitals, Budapest has good nightlife, with a great variety of night spots, from the staid to the near-riotous. The *Troubadour* at the Hilton and the *Starlight* at the Intercontinental are elegant, expensive and somewhat subdued. Other favorites are *Maxim's,* at the Hotel Emke, and the *Moulin Rouge,* in Nagymező Utca; both have good floorshows, both charge an entrance fee and both are expensive. Best reserve. Avoid whiskey, unless you have money to throw around. The *Hungária,* in Lenin Körút, is also very popular, and the *Horoszkóp* at the Buda-Penta hotel is currently considered top favorite.

On Castle Hill the *Old Firenze* is worth a visit, as is the *Casanova,* a few yards from the Danube bank, in Buda. In the Inner City, try the *Anna,* in Váci Utca, or the far-less-sedate *Pipacs,* a few yards away in Aranykéz Utca. The choice and variety are endless—and the scene is constantly changing.

Both discos and nightclubs charge an entrance fee, which ranges, in general, between 30 and 100 Ft. Drinks vary in price from 50 to 120 Ft. in a disco and from 150 to 400 Ft. in a nightclub. A bottle of French champagne costs around 2,200 Ft., Soviet champagne (surprisingly good) about 750 Ft. These prices are, of course, subject to change. A "disco boat" is anchored on the south side of the Chain Bridge, opposite the Forum Hotel.

PARKS AND GARDENS. Budapest is extremely well supplied with large and beautiful parks and gardens—and the Buda Hills themselves are, for the most part, wooded and parklike. Here is a selection of those most worth visiting.

Margaret Island. Almost the whole island is one large park, occupying over 200 acres. It contains vast sports grounds and the National Swimming Pool, as well as Budapest's largest public swimming pool, the Palatinus, with artificial waves, medicinal pools and separate pools for children. This has changing rooms for almost 20,000 visitors. There is also a tennis stadium, an open-air stage and a water tower, built in 1911, which now serves as an observatory. Art is exhibited in the area beneath it. A large new spa-hotel, the Thermal, lies towards the north of the island and an older one, the Grand, nearby, has recently been rebuilt and reopened. There are a number of interesting historic relics, including the remains of a medieval Dominican nunnery and of a 13th-century Franciscan church. Cars and taxis may only enter the island from the north, over Árpád Bridge, but bus 26, starting just off Marx Tér, near the West Station, is permitted to enter from the south. Camping on the island is strictly forbidden.

City Park, (Városliget) in Pest. The largest park in Budapest. It contains the Zoological Garden, a circus and an amusement park. In the center is a large boating lake (where people skate in winter) and, on the shores of the lake, a group of exhibition buildings. The park is easily reached by the subway (underground railway) from the Inner City.

Gellért Hill, in Buda. Though the side facing the Danube is fairly steep, it has been landscaped with stairs, small or large look-out spaces, benches and zigzag paths. The Citadella, or Old Fort, is a pleasant goal with its indoor and outdoor restaurant.

SHOPPING. Almost all shops—and all the larger ones—are state-owned, and the variety of goods on sale, although a vast improvement on even the recent past, is generally somewhat limited. The best things to buy are peasant embroideries, cut glass, and the charming Herend and Zsolnay porcelain. The *Intertourist* shops (which accept only hard currency) have the widest choice. Intertourist has branches all over the city as well as kiosks in most of the hotels. Its main shop is at Kígyó Utca 5, in the Inner City pedestrian shopping precinct. There is also an excellent folk art shop at Váci Utca 14, also in the shopping precinct, and smaller, similar shops in all important streets; in these you can pay in Hungarian currency. Records are also an excellent buy, as are dolls dressed in peasant costume, cut glass, hand-painted pottery and lace. The *Konsumtourist* shop often has interesting objects for sale, up to a hundred years old, for hard currency (e.g. dollars or pounds). It is opposite the Opera, at Népköztársaság Útja 27.

There are first-class, if expensive, fashion shops in Váci Utca and neighboring streets. Hungarian tailors, for both men and women, are also good.

There are so-called "commission shops" (*bizományi boltok*), where such things as antiques and pictures are sold on commission by private persons. You may occasionally find a good piece, but a word of warning! If it is a work of art, you will need a special permit to take it home with you; the shops will advise you on this. But if you buy anything of value from the hard currency shops, you need no such permit; keep the receipt, which will ensure a safe passage through Hungarian customs.

There are a number of privately-owned boutiques in the Váci Utca area, behind the Duna-Intercontinental Hotel, as well as in other parts of the city. Their goods are generally of high quality, with prices to match.

You might like to wander round one of the department stores and here are some of the principal stores of Budapest. Note that service at large stores that are not primarily intended for foreign visitors can at times be offhand. A good rule is that the smaller the store, the more gracious the attention you will receive, though the three-line system–select, pay, collect–still operates in many places. The largest is the *Corvin Áruház* (áruház—department store), Blaha Lujza Tér, just off Rákóczi Út. Others are *Luxus Áruház,* in Vörösmarty Tér, in the Inner City, and three new stores called *Skála Áruház,* one not far from the Gellért Hotel in Buda, another in Óbuda (Old Buda) and the latest and strikingly modern, opposite the West Station. The *Vásárcsarnok* (Central Market), Tolbuhin Körút, near Kálvin Tér, is a colorful covered fruit and vegetable market and ranks high among the interesting sights of Budapest. The best bookshops are in Váci Utca (in the Inner City) and in Népköztársaság Útja.

There are several second-hand bookshops (known as *Antikvárium*); the chief of these are in Múzeum Körút, opposite the National Museum, but there is a well-stocked second-hand shop in Váci Utca, the main shopping street in the Inner City.

The Flea Market (*Ecseri Piac*) is some way out, in Kispest (Nagy kőrösi Út 56).

SIGHTSEEING. There are a number of sightseeing tours by bus, organized by IBUSZ (the state tourist organization) and by Budapest Tourist, which cover all the main sights. Most IBUSZ tours start from the Engels Tér bus terminal, the Budapest Tourist trips from their head office at Roosevelt Square 5, not far away. One 3-hour tour covers all the main sights of the city and runs both morning and afternoon. It costs around $10. There are other tours to the Parliament and the Castle, to museums and galleries, to the Buda Hills and to the Danube Bend. There is also a five-hour-long *Budapest by Night* program. Full details and prices can be obtained from the travel offices mentioned.

For those traveling to or from Vienna, a slightly longer and more expensive (around $50) alternative to the train is highly recommendable. From April to October a hydrofoil goes from Vienna to Budapest (4½ hours) and from Budapest to Vienna (5½ hours—against the current). On some days there are two hydrofoils. It is a comfortable journey with refreshments available and fine views of the Danube Bend, Bratislava and Danube shipping. You can book through IBUSZ or, in Budapest, at the International Ship-Station, Belgrád rakpart, or, in Vienna, at Schiffsstation, Praterkai, Mexico Pl. 8.

USEFUL ADDRESSES. The main embassies are all in Budapest: *British:* Harmincad Utca 6, Budapest V (off Vörösmarty Square); tel: 182–888.

American: Szabadság Tér 12 (near the Parliament); tel: 126–450. *Canadian:* Budakeszi Út 32 (in Buda); tel. 767–711.

The address of the *Hungarian Automobile Club* (*Magyar Autóklub*) is Rómer Flóris Utca 4 (telephone of information desk: 353–101). The Club provides a towing service and other help for motorists. The Club's office is in Buda, near the west end of the Margithíd (Margaret Bridge).

HUNGARY'S HEARTLAND

The Danube Bend

The Danube Bend, where the great river breaks through the Börz-söny and Visegrád mountains, represents a major shift in the flow of the river. It stretches for 19 to 23 km. (12 to 14 miles). But for the tourist the name means a much larger district, both the immediate vicinity of the Danube banks, an area stretching from Esztergom to Budapest, first flowing west to east and then bending near the town of Vác, into a more-or-less direct north to south line, and the mountains that rise along both sides. In the north, this stretches to the Czech border and includes the Börzsöny Mountains; in the south, the hills of Esztergom and Visegrád.

Scenically, it is a most varied part of Hungary. There is a whole chain of riverside spas and watering places, bare volcanic mountains and limestone hills. It is the heartland of Hungary's history. Here the *limes,* the frontier district of the Roman Empire, was established, here kings set up their residences, ambassadors came and great international and national forces met and clashed. The Danube Bend was one of the celebrated centers of the cultural life of the Hungarian Renaissance; it contains archeological and historical relics stretching back six or eight centuries.

The region on the west bank of the Danube is the more interesting, with three charming and picturesque towns—Szentendre, Visegrád and Esztergom—all of which richly repay a visit. The district can be covered by car in one day, the total round trip being no more than 108 km. (67 miles), but this would allow only a cursory look at the many places of interest. Two days, with a night at either Visegrád or Esztergom (both of which have good hotels), would give the visitor time for a more thorough and more leisurely look at this delightful part of Hungary. The east bank has only one town, Vác, and that of only moderate interest, though it also has many pleasant holiday resorts; but it cannot be compared in its appeal to the tourist with the west bank. There are numerous ferries across the Danube, though no bridges, so that it would be possible to combine a visit to both sides of the Danube if the visitor so wished—and had ample time.

Work has started on the building of a hydro-electric dam near Nagymaros, not far from Visegrád. The project was proposed by Czechoslovakia and has been reluctantly agreed to by Hungary, which feels that the water supply to both countries will be adversely affected and that an area of great natural beauty will be ruined.

The West Bank

Whether one leaves Budapest by rail (electric suburban train from Batthyány Tér) or road for Szentendre, the nearest and most picturesque town of the Danube Bend, one sees on the right Aquincum, a Roman settlement dating from the 1st century A.D. and the capital of the Roman province of Pannonia. Little remains of the military settlement, but the civilian city has been well excavated and reconstructed and provides a good example of an important Roman town. The most notable buildings are the basilica, the forum and the public baths.

The Aquincum Museum contains relics of a Roman camp, inscribed stones, mosaics, glass and jewelry. The Hercules Villa, in Meggyfa Utca, just before Aquincum, contains beautiful mosaic floors.

Just beyond Aquincum is the Római fürdő (Roman Bath), one of Budapest's two main campsites.

Szentendre, about 19 km. (12 miles) from Budapest on a good, though very busy, road, is one of the most charming small towns in Hungary, with a population of about 17,000. It was settled by refugees from Serbia and Greece fleeing from the advancing Turks. They built their own Baroque churches, many of them beautifully decorated. The Greek-Orthodox church in the main square, and the Serbian-Orthodox Cathedral on a hill just to the north, are well worth visiting. The little cobble-stoned streets, with their picturesque Baroque houses have an old-world charm. There are several museums, including one displaying the outstanding ceramic work of the late Margit Kovács; this should on no account be missed by pottery enthusiasts. Among other museums perhaps the most interesting is the Szabadtéri Néprajzi Múzeum (Open-Air Ethnographical Museum), about 5 km. (3 miles) to the northwest (direct

bus from the suburban railway station); this contains a collection
showing Hungarian peasant life and folk architecture; it is being
constantly expanded. The town has several good restaurants, some
of which serve Greek and Serbian dishes.

We continue along the west bank of the Danube, past Leány-
falu,a pleasant holiday resort, with a tourist hotel and a campsite,
to Visegrád (43 km./27 miles from Budapest), once the seat of the
kings of Hungary. The town now has less than 3,000 inhabitants,
but in the 14th century it was both large and important. It was
then that the Angevin kings built a citadel here, which became the
royal residence.

Later, King Matthias Corvinus (1458–1490) had a palace built
on the banks of the Danube. Its entrance is in the main street (Fő
Utca). It was razed to the ground by the Turks and it is only since
1934 or so that the ruins have been excavated and much of what
must have been a magnificent palace has been restored. Specially
worthy of a visit is the red marble well, built by a 15th-century
Italian architect, and decorated with the arms of King Matthias.
This is situated in a ceremonial courtyard, which has been restored
in accordance with authentic contemporary records. Above the
courtyard rise the various halls; that on the left has a few fine original carvings, which give an idea of how rich and beautiful the 15th-
century palace must have been. Do not fail to walk or drive up
to the remains of the citadel (good restaurant and hotel at the top),
which provides a superb view.

Esztergom

Esztergom can be reached either by continuing along the Danube bank from Visegrád (64 km./40 miles from Budapest) or directly from the capital by a good road (bus service). In the summer
a so-called "nostalgic" train, drawn by a historic steam locomotive
and with a buffet car, leaves Budapest West station each Saturday
and Sunday morning, returning in the late afternoon, and allowing
six hours for sightseeing in Esztergom. The city, which stands on
the site of a Roman fortress, is the seat of the Cardinal-Primate
of Hungary and its striking cathedral (built 1822–1869) is the largest church in the country. It lies on a hill overlooking the town.
Its most interesting features are the Bakócz chapel (1506–1511),
named after a Primate of Hungary who only narrowly missed becoming Pope—it was part of the earlier medieval church and was
incorporated in the new edifice—and the sacristy, which contains
a valuable collection of medieval ecclesiastical art. According to
tradition, Géza, the father of Hungary's first king, St. Stephen, was
born in Esztergom and it was here that Stephen was crowned, in
1000. Below the Cathedral Hill lies the so-called Víziváros (Water
Town), with many fine Baroque buildings, and here, in the Primate's palace, is the splendid Keresztény Múzeum (Museum of
Christian Art), which is the finest art gallery in Hungary after that

in Budapest and is particularly rich in early Hungarian and Italian paintings and contains, among much else of value, paintings from Duccio's workshop and by Memling and Cranach. A special treasure of the museum is the so-called "Coffin of Our Lord" from Garamszentbenedek, now in Czechoslovakia; the wooden statues of the Apostles and of the Roman soldiers guarding the coffin are masterpieces of Hungarian 15th-century sculpture. There are also fine French tapestries and a French Renaissance codex among the treasures. The same building houses the Primate's Archives, whose oldest document dates from 1187; it contains 40,000 volumes, including several medieval codices and incunabula. To visit the Archives, permission must be obtained in advance. When, in the 17th century, Buda became the political capital of Hungary, Esztergom remained—and still is—the country's ecclesiastical capital.

At Esztergom, the Danube is now the frontier; across the river is Czechoslovakia. The bridge is no longer in existence, though parts of it can still be seen; there is a ferry but it may only be used by the local inhabitants.

The East Bank

The only town of importance on the east bank, Vác, is 35 km. (22 miles) from Budapest and can be reached either by road or rail. Its two chief monuments are its Cathedral, built in 1763–77 by Archbishop Migazzi to the designs of the Italian architect Canevale, and a triumphal arch, by the same architect, erected to celebrate the visit to the town of the Empress Maria Theresa.

Along the Danube north of Vác lie a whole string of pleasant summer resorts, nestling below the picturesque Börzsöny Hills and stretching as far as Szob, just before the Czechoslovak frontier.

PRACTICAL INFORMATION FOR
HUNGARY'S HEARTLAND

TOURIST INFORMATION. The following are the addresses of the local tourist offices. **Szentendre:** near the landing stage; **Visegrád:** Fő Utca (Main Street); **Esztergom:** IBUSZ office, Széchenyi Tér; **Vác:** IBUSZ, Széchenyi Utca.

WHEN TO COME. "Szentendre Days" in July include a symposium on art, concerts of Baroque and modern music, cookery competition, beauty and dancing contests, campfire programs on the Danube embankment. A revival of the traditional market-day theatrical performances takes place in the Main Square (Marx Tér). Throughout July, some newly-discovered classic of Hungarian drama and folk poetry is performed against the background of the old medieval and Baroque houses: *commedia dell'arte* productions with close contact between audience and players. The "Szentendre Spring Days," held at the end of March, provide a program of music and folklore.

GETTING AROUND. If you have enough time, you should certainly travel by boat from Budapest, a leisurely and pleasant journey, especially in summer and spring. The steamers for Esztergom start from the main Pest landing stage near Vigadó Tér. On summer Sundays and public holidays a hydrofoil service brings Visegrád within an hour, and Esztergom within under two hours of Budapest. Timetables available at your hotel. Trains run frequently to Szentendre from Batthyány Tér, in Buda. By car via Szentendre-Visegrád, follow no. 11 highway, which more or less hugs the Buda bank of the Danube. A day-long coach tour is run by IBUSZ in the season on Tuesdays, Fridays and Saturdays, visiting Szentendre, Visegrád and Esztergom; including lunch and wine tasting, it costs around $22. Strongly recommended. For special steam train at weekends in the season, see page 255.

To reach Vác, go by steamer from Budapest, Vigadó Square, by bus or train from the West Station, or by road via highway no. 2.

HOTELS AND RESTAURANTS

Esztergom. *Esztergom* (M), (tel. 81–68); on the island in the Danube. *Fürdő* (M), (tel. 292); attached to the local spa and swimming pools. *Volán* (I), (tel. 271), in the town center, near the park. *Vadvirág,* guest house. Campsite; paying-guest accommodations.

Restaurants. *Kispipa,* Kossuth Utca. Halászcsárda (fisherman's inn), on the island. *Csülök,* in the town center.

Szentendre. *Danubius* (M), (tel. 12–511); *Party* (I), (tel. 12–491); *Sziget* (I), (tel. 10–697), all attractive hotels on the Danube bank north of the town. Guest houses; tourist-hostel; campsites; paying-guest accommodations.

Restaurants. *Arany Sárkány,* near town center, warmly recommended. *Béke,* in main square, *Görög Kancsó,* on Danube bank, and many others.

Vác. No recommended hotel; guesthouse and paying-guest accommodations.

Restaurants. *Halászkert* (fish restaurant) on Danube bank; *Fehér Galamb,* Lenin Út; snack bar in Széchenyi Utca.

Visegrád. *Silvanus* (M), (tel. 136–063) on top of Mount Visegrád, with a spectacular view; highly recommended, especially for motorists. *Vár,* (tel. 28–264) in the main street, offers simple accommodations. Also bungalows, campsites and paying-guest accommodations.

Restaurants. *Vár Étterem,* in main street; *Diófa, Sirály,* both near Danube.

LAKE BALATON

The Nation's Playground

Lake Balaton is the largest lake in Central Europe. It stretches some 80 km. (50 miles) across Western Hungary, within easy reach of Budapest. The 193 km. (120 miles) of its shoreline are almost completely occupied by a continuous chain of summer resorts. The southern shore is generally flat, with long sandy beaches and only an occasional steep hill rising from the lake, as at Fonyód; the northern shore is marked by a chain of long-extinct, eroded volcanoes, of which the Badacsony is the largest and the most remarkable. The peninsula of Tihany sweeps deep into the lake and brings the two shores quite close. The water of the southern shore is very shallow and warms up to a remarkable degree; you can walk for almost a mile before it deepens, and thus it is ideal for children. On the northern shore it shelves more abruptly and the swimming is better, though the water is also pleasantly warm even in autumn and spring.

In recent years much has been done to develop the lake into a mass recreation area. Most of the private villas and hotels have been nationalized and turned into trade union and factory holiday homes. (Hungarian writers, for instance, have an attractive literary retreat at Szigliget.) At the same time, new hotels have been built and more are being planned, with tourist hostels, students' homes and large camping sites in many places. Many privately owned villas have been built, often to be let to visitors during the season. During the three summer months, the whole lakeshore is extremely crowded. The wise visitor will choose either the late spring or the often incredibly beautiful fall for his stay, when prices are somewhat lower and he will find much more elbow room.

The Balaton has much to offer in water sports. Swimming, sailing, and windsurfing are all catered for—you can hire boats and boards. Motorboats are forbidden, however. There are numerous cottages for anglers (though note that April 25 to May 25 is closed season for fishing). During the winter, skating, ice-sailing and ice-fishing are especially popular. There is a special sled used on the Balaton ice known as the *fakutya* (wooden dog). Among the non-aquatic sports, various ball games are the best catered for. International fencing championships are held every year near the lake.

The Balaton is extremely well provided with both road and rail communications. In the summer, frequent fast trains run from Budapest and there are through trains from most parts of Hungary. On summer Saturdays there is a through express from Vienna to Siófok and back. Long-distance bus services connect it with every part of the country. The new M7 motorway runs from Budapest to Zamárdi, west of Siófok; it bypasses some major resorts, but is connected to them by link-roads. The lake is crisscrossed by frequent ferry-boats, which provide the most leisurely and pleasant way of exploring its shores.

The Southern Shore

Along the whole of this shore, from Balatonaliga in the east to Balatonberény in the west, there is a practically unbroken chain of summer resorts. Here are the "mass," popular, crowded beaches which attract most local and foreign visitors. But there are smaller, quieter, places, too, with an unpretentious informality of their own. It is on this shore that the family hotels and the children's holiday homes have largely been developed.

The nearest resorts to Budapest are Balatonaliga and Balatonvilágos, on the easternmost corner of the lake. Like all the places on the southern shore, they are served by the Budapest-Nagykanizsa railway, while the M7 motorway approaches the lake at Balatonvilágos, which is connected to it by a link-road. There are no hotels at either place, but ample paying-guest accommodations are available, as well as a campsite; there are plenty of snack bars and cafes.

Siófok

Siófok is the largest and by far the most popular community on the southern shore. It has a well-developed tourist organization and a long row of comfortable and pleasant modern hotels, all overlooking the lake. Its history stretches back a long time; the Ro-

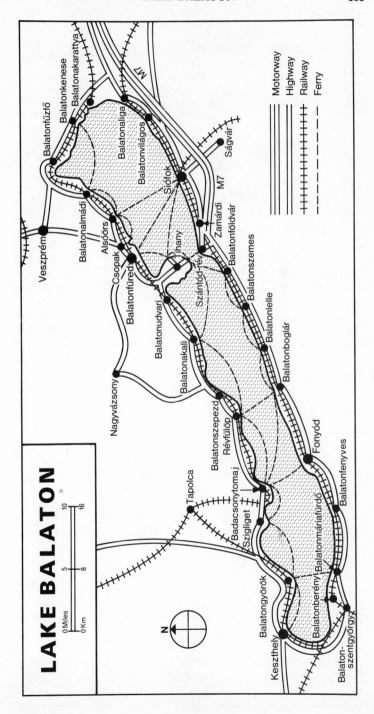

mans had already settled here and had built locks to regulate the level of the lake at the mouth of the river Sió. Nonetheless, there is little to see in the town itself. The József Beszédes Múzeum in Sió Utca contains displays of the history of Balaton shipping and there is a library and a large open-air theater, which seats 1,800. But the main attraction is the long, sandy beach, where most of the "action" is, and the pleasant, shady gardens with their open-air restaurants.

There is one excursion of interest to be made from Siófok; along highway 65 we can reach Ságvár (nine km./six miles), which has Roman remains, those of the fortified camp of Tricciani (284–305 A.D.). In the clay soil of the surrounding hills, traces of primitive man's occupation 17,000 years old have been found.

Zamárdi, a few kilometers further on, is a quiet resort. It is here that the M7 motorway reaches the lakeside, having passed just south of Siófok. The village has restaurants and cafes. To the west of it, towards the neighboring resort of Szántód-Rév, there is a campsite for motorists with its own 731-meter (800-yard) long beach, snack bar, general store and a pleasant garden-restaurant within walking distance. There are also rowing boats for hire. Zamárdi village has a few fine old peasant houses and there are ancient wine-cellars among the nearby vineyards. The baroque church dates from 1771–74. A walk of less than three hours takes us to Balatonendréd, a small village with some striking Roman remains; the community is known for its exquisite lace-making.

Szántód-Rév is at the narrowest point of Lake Balaton; the ferries to Tihany, on the northern shore, start here, taking only eight minutes. At the ferry-landing stands the old Rév (Ferry) Inn, recently and lovingly restored, with a wine room and a nearby snack bar. Close by is Szántódpuszta, with its restaurant, horseriding and trips on oxdrawn carts.

Balatonföldvár

Balatonföldvár is one of the oldest-established resorts on the southern shore of the lake. Designed and laid out around the end of the 19th century, it has a large park, promenades, many picturesque villas and excellent bathing beaches. The Fenyves (Pine) Park has an open-air theater. Three km. (two miles) or so to the south (there is a bus service) lies the village of Kőröshegy, which has a 15th-century single-naved Gothic church, restored in the 20th century but retaining many of its original features. Recitals of music by Bach, Liszt and Kodály are given in the church in the summer.

Balatonszárszó is another of the quiet, peaceful resorts, with a few charming little inns, restaurants and cafes. There is a good beach. It was here that Attila József, one of Hungary's greatest modern poets, killed himself in 1937 by throwing himself in front of a train. There is a memorial museum in the street called after him and the park contains a bronze statue of him.

Balatonszemes is another old-established lakeside resort, situated partly on the shore and partly inland. The former Hunyady mansion (built in the second half of the 18th century), the Gothic church (15th century) and the so-called Bagolyvár (Owl's Castle), which stands on the site of an old Turkish fort, are all worth visiting.

Balatonlelle is one of the busiest resorts on the southern shore. There are well-appointed beaches and much traffic at the ferry-boat pier. In the village there are one or two fine old houses. The annual meeting of Hungarian folk artists takes place here.

Balatonboglár, now administratively united with Balatonlelle under the name of Boglárlelle, was mentioned as a community as early as the 13th century. There are good beaches and much ferry traffic, with a direct line to Révfülöp on the northern shore. There is a wine research station in the village, which has a number of picturesque old houses.

Fonyód

Fonyód is the furthest from Budapest of the major resorts on the southern bank of the lake. It consists of several different settlements, stretching seven km. (over four miles). It is growing rapidly and is being developed as the most important bathing resort on the southern shore after Siófok. It is an ancient settlement; historical discoveries include late Stone Age and Bronze Age implements and there are Roman ruins. Fonyód began to be developed around 1890; since the 1930s it has been one of the most popular places on the lake's southern side; its steep wooded hills and its altogether charming situation, combined with its excellent beaches, are ensuring an ever-greater influx of visitors. An interesting excursion can be made to Buzsák, some 16 km. (about ten miles) to the south, a village famous for its colorful folk art and for its fine carvings, mostly done by shepherds.

Balatonmáriafürdő is another small, quiet resort, set among vineyards; its excellent beach stretches along ten km. (six miles) of the lake shore. There are good accommodations, as well as a restaurant and nightclub.

At Balatonberény, the last resort on the southern shore, the lake narrows and there is a fine view of the Keszthely Hills, on the opposite side. The village was settled under the Árpád dynasty and Bronze Age and Roman relics have been found here. The Roman Catholic church dates from the 15th century; its original Gothic design was remodeled into Baroque in the 18th. There is a nudist campsite here.

The Northern Shore

This is different in many ways from the southern shore of the lake. The geographical structure is less uniform and the outlying spurs of the Bakony Hills and the extinct volcanoes of the Tapolca Basin make it a romantic, often dramatic, landscape. The almost flat southern shore provides little beyond one continuous sandy beach and caters for large crowds; the northern shore, on the other hand, is more "select," more fashionable; it, too, has several fine beaches, but it has also many other attractions and many interesting objectives for excursions into the hinterland, with its ruined castles, charming valleys, forests and springs.

The water of the Balaton is just as soft and enticing as on the opposite shore, but the beaches shelve much more sharply and are, on the whole, less suitable for children, demanding swimming rather than playful splashing about. Here and there the bottom is sandy, but in places it is pebbly and stony.

Balatonakarattya and Balatonkenese are the first resorts on the northern shore to be reached by a traveler from Budapest. They lie on gentle hill slopes covered with vineyards and have campsites, bungalows, restaurants and cafes, as well as several good beaches.

Balatonfűzfő, on the northernmost corner of the lake, is surrounded on the landward side by hills and woods. Though it has a beach, it is now above all an industrial community, with paper mills and a chemical factory. However, the village has an Olympic-sized covered swimming pool, the only one of its kind in the Balaton area; it is the venue of international events.

Balatonalmádi has developed into a town of some size, with many good shops, restaurants and places of entertainment; the excellent beach is one of the best on the northern shore of the lake. Buses ply to neighboring resorts and to the picturesque town of Veszprém (see chapter on Western Hungary), and there is a boat pier.

The next resort is Alsóörs, a quiet, beautifully-situated village. It has a campsite, bungalows and an inn. At Felsőörs, a few miles to the north, is the finest Romanesque church of the Balaton uplands, as well as an 18th-century priory.

Csopak is situated on the hillside, the resort stretching down to the lake. It lies in fine wine-growing country; the beach is well supplied with all the usual holiday amenities. Paying-guest accommodations are available and there are two pleasant inns. The former Ranolder castle, dating from the middle of the 19th century, now houses the Institute for Plant Protection.

Balatonfüred

Balatonfüred is the oldest, most distinguished and most internationally famous health resort of this shore of the lake. It has every amenity of a lakeside holiday resort and is, in addition, a spa of the first class. Above the beaches and the promenade the twisting streets of the old town climb the hillsides, which are thickly planted with vines. The hills protect the town from cold northerly winds. This is one of the most celebrated wine-growing districts of Hungary and it frames an old-established spa for cardiac diseases. Great plane and poplar trees provide shade as you arrive by boat at the always-busy landing-stage.

The center of the town in Gyógy Tér (Spa Square), where the waters of the volcanic springs bubble and rise under a slim, colonnaded pavilion. The springs have a strong carbonic content. In the Square is the Cardiac Hospital, where hundreds of patients from all over the world are treated.

Balatonfüred has 11 medicinal springs and they have a stimulating and highly-beneficial effect on the heart and nerves. There is plenty of sunshine but also pleasant shade. It was here that Rabindranath Tagore, the great Indian poet and Nobel Prize winner, recovered from a heart attack. He planted a tree to commemorate his stay, a tree which still stands in a little park of its own. Another Nobel Prize winner, the Italian poet Salvatore Quasimodo, planted his own tree near Tagore's in 1961.

There is much to see in and around Balatonfüred and an excursion to Tihany (described later on) should on no account be missed. There is a classical Round church (Kerek templom), built in 1841–46, near the center of the town and there are many picturesque old houses as well as an attractive ensemble of neo-Classical villas around Gyógy Tér. There are several beaches.

The most interesting longer excursion, apart from that to Tihany, already mentioned, is to the small town of Nagyvázsony, about 19 km. (12 miles) to the northwest. Its castle was built in the 15th century and owned by Pál Kinizsi, one of the generals of King Matthias Corvinus and known for his great physical strength. In late July and early August a colorful equestrian pageant in medieval costumes is held in the grounds of the former Zichy Castle in the town (now a "country-house hotel").

Tihany

The small peninsula of Tihany, surrounded on three sides by the lake, is a rich open-air museum as well as a very popular holiday resort. There are geological and botanical rarities; the Celtic walls of the Óvár (Old Castle), the ruins of the Roman watchtower on Csúcshegy (Mount Peak), the traces of churches dating back to the Árpád dynasty, the squat Romanesque columns of the 900-year-old Abbey crypt—all bear witness to human faith and human hate.

From the ferry on the lakeside the road climbs between poplars to the range of hills which form the peninsula; these are barely 200 meters (650 ft.) high and are covered with acacia copses. Only a few hundred yards beyond the "Club Tihany" tourist complex, nature appears primitive and undisturbed. In the middle of the peninsula, framed in waving green reeds, is the smooth Belső (Inner) Lake. Around it are bare, yellowish-white rocks; volcanic cones rise against the sky. The whole area, so rich in rare flora and fauna, is a national park, where all building and agriculture are carefully controlled.

Between the Inner Lake and the eastern shore of the peninsula lies the village of Tihany, with, as its crowning glory, the famous Abbey. Its foundations were laid by King Andrew I some nine centuries ago. Only the crypt, in which the king is buried, and a priceless historical document have survived the ravages of time. This document, the Abbey charter, dating from 1055, contains in its Latin text many Hungarian words and phrases—one of the earliest surviving documents to do so. It is kept at Pannonhalma; see Western Hungary chapter. The present Abbey church is in a Baroque style and was built between 1719 and 1737; it is magnificently ornate, with silver-gilt altars and, on the large ceiling fresco, pink floating angels. The Abbey has a famous organ, on which recitals are given in the summer. It also houses a museum and is visited each year by over 100,000 people. In the village there are many beautiful old houses, the finest of which have been formed into an open-air museum. Tihany has a Biological Research Institute and an Institute of Geophysics, with an observatory.

There is no railway station at Tihany, but it is easily reached by a regular bus service from Balatonfüred or by one of the frequent ferry boats.

Going westwards along the northern shore of the lake, we come to Örvényes, a quiet resort with an 18th-century watermill, which holds an exhibition of folk art, and a Baroque Roman Catholic church. A few miles further on is Balatonudvari, with a breeding-station for Balaton fish. The beach is at Kiliántelep, about a mile to the west; here there is a large campsite with a self-service restaurant, a motel and a supermarket.

Révfülöp is a traditional crossing point of the southern basin of the lake; there are around eight ferry boats a day to and from Balatonboglár, on the southern shore, as well as ferries to most of the other lakeside resorts. There is a campsite here, and a small hotel, as well as paying-guest accommodations and a restaurant. One of the prettiest villages of the Balaton is Kővágóörs, a few miles inland. Another campsite is a few miles further along the shore, at Pálköve, near the rail station of Balatonrendes. This, together with the adjoining Ábrahámhegy, forms one of the quieter resorts of the northern Balaton. It has excellent local wines. There is a small motel and a pleasant restaurant.

The Badacsony

Along the volcanic, cone-shaped peaks of the Balaton Uplands, the broad-beamed, flat-topped Badacsony is one of the most striking. The masses of lava that coagulated here created bizarre and beautiful rock formations. At the upper edge there are 180- to 200-foot- (52- to 61-meter) high basalt columns in a huge semicircle. The land around has been lovingly tilled for centuries and everywhere there are vineyards and in every inn and tavern there is splendid wine. The Badacsony is now a protected area.

Badacsonytomaj is a holiday resort with several restaurants and cafes, as well as a well-known winetasting bar (the Borkóstoló). On the top of the mountain is the Kisfaludy House, named after the Hungarian poet Sándor Kisfaludy (1772–1844), who lived here. It has a fine view. The picturesque Baroque wine-press house belonging to the poet's wife, Róza Szegedi, is now a museum. There is also a wine museum, illustrating the history of local wines and of Hungarian wines generally.

Szigliget is a small village at the foot of the Várhegy (Castle Hill), which rises more than 183 meters (600 ft.) above the lake. The resort has a good beach, a campsite and a ferry landing-stage.

Keszthely

Keszthely is the second-largest town on the Balaton. It has a municipal charter dating from 1404; its Romanesque Roman Catholic parish church was built in 1386; and its famous agricultural college, the Georgikon, was established in 1797. The town offers the rare combination of a historical center of culture and a restful summer resort.

The magnificent Baroque Festetics Palace, begun around 1750, is one of the finest in Hungary. Concerts are held in the fine music room or, in the summer, in the courtyard. The palace is surrounded by a beautiful park. The Helikon Library, in the south wing of the palace, contains over 50,000 volumes, as well as precious incunabula, a collection of etchings and valuable paintings. The Georgikon, now the Agricultural University, has become the agricultural headquarters of southwestern Hungary. The Balaton Museum contains rich and varied exhibits of local history, ethnography, folk art and painting.

Keszthely has excellent hotel accommodations in all categories, good restaurants, cafes and pastry shops; it has several good beaches and opportunities for every kind of sport.

At Fenekpuszta, about eight km. (five miles) south of Keszthely, lie ruins of the Roman town of Valcum and an early Christian basilica. Some six km (four miles) to the northwest of Keszthely is the spa town of Hévíz. It has excellent hotels and a casino. Another popular spa is Zalakaros, southwest of Keszthely.

The Little Balaton (Kis-Balaton)

The largest river feeding the Balaton, the Zala, enters the lake at its southernmost point. On either side there is a swamp of several thousand acres, formerly part of the lake. This is now a vast protected area and the home of many rare birds. The area can be visited only by special permission, obtainable from the Országos Környezet és Természetvédelmi Hivatal (National Office for the Protection of Nature), Költő Utca 21–23, Budapest XII.

PRACTICAL INFORMATION FOR LAKE BALATON

WHEN TO COME. If you like crowds and the best of the summer sun, choose June, July and August. Spring or fall are less crowded and prices are lower. Winter is the time to go for skating, ice-sailing and ice-fishing.

Southern Shore

TOURIST INFORMATION. The following are the addresses of the local tourist offices. **Balatonboglár:** Dózsa György Utca 13; **Balatonföldvar:** Hősök Útja 9; **Balatonlelle:** Szent István Utca 1; **Fonyód:** next to the station; **Siófok:** adjoining station and in main street Fő Utca).

GETTING AROUND. All the resorts on the southern shore are either on, or just off, the M7 highway or its continuation Highway 7. By rail, they all lie on the main Budapest-Nagykanizsa line, most of the trains of which leave the South Station (Déli pályaudvar) in Budapest. Regular ferry connections link main resorts on the lake itself.

HOTELS AND RESTAURANTS

All hotels listed below have restaurants unless otherwise stated.

Balatonboglár. *Platán* (I), (tel. 561), simple. Campsite and paying-guest accommodations.
Restaurants. *Hullám, Kinizsi* (beer hall).

Balatonföldvár. *Neptun* (M), (tel. 40–388), in park near lake. *Fesztival* (I), (tel. 40–377), also near lake. *Juventus* (I), (tel. 40–379), intended for young people—self-catering villas, campsites, paying-guest accommodations.
Restaurants. *Balatongyöngye,* Szentgyörgyi Út. *Kukorica,* Budapesti Út. Self-service restaurants; wine bars.

Balatonlelle. For hotel, see Balatonboglár, above. Campsite, paying-guest accommodations. Several small restaurants, some self-service.

Balatonszárszó. Guest-house; tourist-hostel; bungalows; campsite near the rail station; paying-guest accommodations.
Restaurants. *Tóparti,* on beach; *Vén Diófa,* Kossuth Utca.

Fonyód. *Sirály* (I), in Bartók Béla Utca, above the town (tel. 60–125). Guest
houses, tourist hostels; campsites; paying-guest accommodations.
Restaurants. *Présház* (wine bar), *Vadásztanya.* Several self-service restaurants.

Siófok. *Balaton* (M), (tel. 10–655); *Európa* (M), (tel. 13–411); *Hungária* (M), (tel. 10–677); *Lidó* (M), (tel. 10–633), four large and comfortable hotels on the lake shore. *Napfény* (I), (tel. 11–408), also overlooking the lake; private baths. *Vénusz* (I), (tel. 10–660), in the town.
There is a motel by the lakeside; guest house; tourist-hostel; campsites; paying-guest accommodations.
Restaurants. A large choice; we recommend *Fogas,* in the main street, with garden; *Csárdás,* also in the main street, with gypsy music in the evenings; and *Matróz,* near the pier. Among the numerous night haunts the *Pipacs,* the *Eden,* the *Maxim* and the *Delta* all offer local wines and a live show.

Northern Shore

TOURIST INFORMATION. The following are the addresses of the local tourist offices. **Badacsony:** near the landing stage; **Balatonalmádi:** Lenin Utca and at rail station in summer; **Balatonfüred:** at rail station and in town center; **Hévíz;** Rákóczi Utca; **Keszthely:** Fő Tér. **Tihany:** near the landing stage.

GETTING AROUND. Highway 71 runs the whole length of the northern shore; it branches off the M7 motorway from Budapest some miles to the east of the lake. By rail, there is a good direct service to all the resorts on the north of the lake from Budapest South. Tihany and Hévíz have no railway stations; for Tihany one must get out at Balatonfüred and for Hévíz at Keszthely; in both cases there are frequent connecting buses. Regular ferry connections link main resorts on the lake itself.

HOTELS AND RESTAURANTS

All hotels listed below have restaurants unless otherwise stated.

Badacsony. *Egri József* tourist-hostel; guest houses, campsite, paying-guest accommodations.
Restaurants. *Bormúzeum* (wine-tasting), *Halászkert* (garden restaurant specializing in fish), *Kisfaludi Ház.*

Balatonalmadi. *Auróra* (M), (tel. 38–811). *Tulipán* (I), (tel. 38–317). *Kék Balaton* tourist-hostel; motel; campsite; paying-guest accommodations.
Restaurants. *Aranyhíd, Kakascsárda, Muskátli;* self-service restaurant on the beach.

Balatonfüred. *Annabella* (tel. 42–222) and *Marina* (tel. 43–644), both (M), are two fine modern hotels on the lakeside. The *Margaréta* apartment-house (tel. 43–824), also (M), is for self-catering; its guests use the beach and other facilities of the *Marina,* which it adjoins.

Arany Csillag (I), (tel. 43–466), old-fashioned hotel in town center with no private baths. Guest houses; bungalows; splendid campsite; paying-guest accommodations.

Restaurants. *Balaton,* in the park; *Baricska, Hordó,* both near the lake. The *Kedves* pastry shop, in Blaha Lujza Utca, serves excellent tea, coffee and cakes in elegant surroundings.

Hévíz. *Aqua* (E), (tel. 11–090). Large luxurious spa hotel. *Thermál* (E), (tel. 11–190), with casino for hard currency. *Napsugár* (M), (tel. 13–208). Guest houses, paying-guest accommodations.

Restaurants. *Kulacs, Piroska, Tokaj-Hegyalja* and many others.

Keszthely. *Helikon* (M–E), (tel. 11–330), large and comfortable new hotel on the lakeside. *Phoenix* (I), (tel. 12–630), next to the Helikon, whose amenities its guests can use. *Amazon,* (tel. 12–448), simple tourist hostel in town center. Several campsites; paying-guest accommodations.

Restaurants. *Béke,* in the main street, simple but good. *Halászcsárda* (fish), on the lakeside; and many others. The *Helikon Tavern,* 8 km. (five miles) east on Highway 71, occupies a neo-Classical building built in the early 19th century by Prince Festetics; open evenings only, all the year round, with a good choice of wines and a gypsy band.

Nagyvázsony. *Kastély* (I), (tel. 31–029), a simple "country-house hotel" in the former Zichy castle; some private baths, pleasant restaurant; riding facilities. Motel; riding-school; tourist-hostel; paying-guest accommodations; several small restaurants.

Tihany. *"Club Tihany complex,"* near the landing-stage, comprising the *Tihany Hotel* (E), (tel. 48–088) and the *"Tihany Holiday Village"* (E), same telephone number, with luxury bungalows; restaurants, tennis courts, squash and minigolf. Paying-guest accommodations.

Restaurants. *Fogas, Sport,* and others. There is a good pastry shop, the *Rege,* near the Abbey.

Zalakaros. *Thermál* (I), (tel. 18–202); bungalows, campsite, paying-guest accommodations.

NORTHERN HUNGARY

Small Mountains, Great Beauty

Northern Hungary is the region which stretches from the Danube north of Budapest to the northeastern borders of the country, to Czechoslovakia and the Soviet Union. It is a clearly defined area, marked by several mountain ranges of no great height but considerable scenic beauty; these form the southernmost outcrops of the Carpathians. Most of them are limestone hills with some volcanic rocks. Few of the peaks reach 914 meters (3,000 ft.) and most of them are thickly wooded almost to their summits. Oak, beech, and hornbeam are the main forest trees, with comparatively few patches of pine and fir. Naturalists, botanists, geologists, ethnographers and folklorists find much of interest in the hills. In the state game reserves herds of deer and wild boar roam freely; the eagle and the rare red-footed falcon still survive.

Within this region most of Hungary's mineral wealth is concentrated—iron, some copper, and rich (though inferior) coal deposits.

The Northern Hills

Historically, the valleys of Northern Hungary have always been of considerable strategic importance, as they provided the only access to the north. Eger, renowned in Magyar feats of arms as one of the guardians of these strategic routes, is in this region, while many ruined castles sit picturesquely on the hilltops. The Mátra mountains, easily reached from Budapest, have been developed into an important winter sports area. Last but not least, this is one of the great wine-growing districts of Hungary, with Gyöngyös and Eger contributing the "Magyar nectar" and (most famous of all) Tokaj producing the "king of wines."

We have already mentioned the Börzsöny Hills in our "Danube Bend" section; they contain many of the most delightful country resorts near Budapest, most of which can be easily reached by the Budapest-Vác-Szob railway line or by bus. Dotted throughout the region are the ruins of many old castles. Nógrád Castle was originally built under the Árpád dynasty; its ancient tower is still a landmark. In the Nógrád valley, which runs between the Nógrád and Mátra Hills are the Palóc villages, representing one of the most interesting and individual ethnic groups of Hungary. In their villages, Hungarian national costumes have been preserved and are still occasionally worn; Hollókő, recently included in UNESCO's World Heritage conservation scheme, is the most picturesque of these.

The Mátra, a volcanic mountain group, rises with dramatic suddenness above the Palóc world. The capital is Gyöngyös, famous for the excellent wine produced round about—do not miss *Debrői hárslevelű*, a magnificent white wine—and, more recently, for its new industrial importance. Early in the 1960s huge lignite deposits were discovered and the large-scale mines and power-stations established since then have changed the character of the whole region. Among the chief sights of the town are the 14th-century church of Szent Bertalan (St. Bartholomew) and the Mátra Museum, which exhibits folk art of the region. To the north of Gyöngyös lie many beautiful resorts, popular in summer for their invigorating mountain air and in winter for their skiing and other seasonable sports. The most famous is Mátrafüred (400 meters/1,312 ft.). Bus services connect the resorts with Gyöngyös and Budapest. The highest peak is Kékestető (1,015 meters/3,330 ft.), the highest point in Hungary, with a sanatorium.

About 11 km. (eight miles) west of Gyöngyös is the charming village of Gyöngyöspata, with a beautifully restored 12th–13th-century church, with frescoes and a unique altar-piece showing the Tree of Jesse. About 24 km. (15 miles) still further west, along minor roads, lies Szirák, with one of the most attractive of Hungary's "country-house hotels." It dates from the late 17th-century and is situated in a fine park.

Highway 3 (a motorway—M3—as far as the town of Gyöngyös) is the main road link between Budapest and Northern Hungary.

Eger

The famous and picturesque city of Eger lies on the line where plain and mountain meet, between the Mátra mountains and their eastern neighbor, the Bükk. It bears within its limits much of the history, the heartbreak and the glory of Hungary's past and should on no account be missed. Eger was settled very early in the Hungarian conquest of the country and one of the five bishoprics founded by King Stephen was here. Eger castle was built after the devastating Tartar invasion and the cathedral, originally Romanesque, was rebuilt in Gothic style in the 15th century, though few vestiges of this structure now remain.

In 1551 the city was attacked by the Turks, but the commander, István Dobó, held out against vastly superior forces. It fell in 1596 and was until 1687 one of the most important northern outposts of Muslim power. The main aspects of present-day Eger were developed in the 18th century and it is now a splendid example of a Baroque city. The imposing Cathedral was completely rebuilt, in Classical style, early in the 19th century; it is the second-largest church in Hungary. Opposite the Cathedral is the former Lyceum, an impressive Baroque building which is now a teachers' training college and includes an observatory.

The most picturesque street of Eger is Kossuth Lajos Utca, which consists almost entirely of Baroque and Rococo buildings. No. 4 is the Minor Canons' residence and one of the most beautiful Rococo palaces in Hungary. Further on, the County Council Hall dates from 1749–56; it has exquisite wrought-iron gates. To the north, in Dobó István Square, stands the fine Baroque Minorite Church. Continuing northwards we reach one of Eger's landmarks, the Turkish minaret. The Castle is best reached along Kossuth Lajos Street, turning to the left at the end; the original casemates survive and much excavation is being carried out. The Castle Museum is worth a visit. Eger is also a spa, with valuable therapeutic waters and bathing facilities of all kinds; the water is recommended for rheumatic ailments.

Eger wine is famous and perhaps the best known is *Bikavér* (Bull's Blood), a full-blooded red wine; *Leányka,* a delightful white wine, and the Eger version of *Medoc Noir,* a heavy, sweet dessert wine, are also outstanding.

A particularly pleasant excursion from Eger is to Szilvásvárad, a charming small resort deep in the wooded Bükk Mountains, some 28 km. (17 miles) north of Eger and easily reached by train or bus. Its streams are full of trout and there are many small waterfalls. Here is the famous Lippizaner stud; there are also facilities for horse riding.

Mezőkövesd, about 16 km. (10 miles) to the southeast, is famous for its folk art, examples of which are on display in the village museum; many of them are for sale.

Miskolc

East of the picturesque Bükk Mountains lies Miskolc, the second-largest town in Hungary and one of its chief industrial centers. A vast conurbation with a population of some 200,000, it is surrounded by beautiful country. It contains some interesting buildings, many of them Baroque, and, in a western suburb, the medieval castle of Diósgyőr. South of the city is the spa-suburb of Miskolc-Tapolca, with the town's best hotels.

Beyond Miskolc lie two objectives of the greatest interest to the visitor; the vast cave system of Aggtelek and the vineyards of Tokaj.

Aggtelek

One of the most extensive cave systems in Europe lies at the extreme northern end of Hungary, right on the Czechoslovak border. The caves are spectacular in the extreme and have been ranked with such natural monuments as the Grand Canyon or the Niagara Falls. The largest of the caves, the Baradla, is 24 km. (over 15 miles) long, with stalactite and stalagmite formations of great beauty and extraordinary size, some more than 45 meters (80 ft.) high. A full tour of the caves takes five hours, but there are shorter tours taking one to two hours, which will give the visitor a very good overall impression of the majesty of this underground marvel of nature. In one of the chambers of the cave a concert-hall has been created; it can hold 1,000 people and concerts are given here. Further caves are being discovered and opened to the public. There are two entrances, at Aggtelek and Jósvafő.

Sárospatak, some 70 km. (45 miles) to the northeast of Miskolc, is the cultural center of this part of Hungary. It is a picturesque old town, with many fine old houses. Its ancient castle was begun in the 11th century and contains a museum of old furniture. Its Calvinist College was founded in 1531 and for many years had close links with Britain. In the 18th century King George II of England took a personal interest in the college and, for about 50 years, education was conducted in both English and Hungarian. Many famous Hungarians were educated here. It is now a state school.

Tokaj

Tokaj, the home of Hungary's most famous wine, lies about 48 km. (30 miles) east of Miskolc. The countryside round it is beautiful, especially in October, when the grapes hang from the vines in thick clusters. Tokay, the "king of wines," as it has been called, is golden yellow with slightly brownish tints and it has an almost oily texture. It has been cultivated for over 700 years. Other countries—France, Germany and Russia—have tried to produce the wine from Tokaj grapes; all failed. It would seem that the secret of the wine lies in a combination of the volcanic soil and the climate. The little town of Tokaj is built on the slopes and contains many wine-cellars. In the Museum of Local History objects connected with the history of the production of the wine are on display.

PRACTICAL INFORMATION FOR
NORTHERN HUNGARY

TOURIST INFORMATION. The following are the addresses of the local tourist offices. **Aggtelek:** at the entrance to the Baradla cave. **Eger:** Bajcsy-Zsilinszky Utca and in the Castle; **Gyöngyös:** Szabadság Tér; **Miskolc:** Széchenyi Utca; **Sárospatak:** Kossuth Utca; **Tokaj:** Bem J. Utca 44.

WHEN TO COME. Spring and summer are the best seasons for the hill resorts. The traditional and extremely colorful wine festivals are held in the fall, when the weather can also be quite delightful.

GETTING AROUND. There are good rail connections from Budapest (East Station). Local trains and buses complete the network. Otherwise, traveling by car gives you the greatest freedom.

HOTELS AND RESTAURANTS

All hotels listed below have restaurants unless otherwise stated.

Aggtelek. *Cseppkő* (I), (tel. 7), very simple. At Jósvafő is the equally simple *Hotel Tengerszem* (tel. 49). Tourist-hostel; campsite; paying-guest accommodations.

Eger. *Eger* (M), in part recently constructed, and *Park* (M), close together and sharing the same telephone number (13–233); the Eger is perhaps short on charm, if up-to-date; the Park is elegant, but rather old-fashioned. Both have rooms with bath. *Unicornis* (I), (tel. 12–886). Several guest houses; motel; campsites; paying-guest accommodations.
Restaurants. *Fehér Szarvas,* adjoining Park Hotel; game. *Kazamata,* Martírok Tere. *Mecset,* Knézich Utca; and many others.
The town has many wine-tasting bars and shops.

Gyöngyös. *Mátra* (M), (tel. 12–057), in town center. Paying-guest accommodations. At Mátrafüred, in the hills some miles north of the town, is the *Avar* (tel. 13–195). Motel, two campsites; private accommodations.
Restaurants. *Kékes,* in main square. *Olimpia;* many wine bars. There are restaurants and snack bars in all the Mátra hill resorts.

Miskolc. *Pannonia* (M), (tel. 88–022). Refurbished, in town center. *Arany Csillag* (tel. 35–114) and *Avas* (tel. 37–798), both (I), and old fashioned.

In the spa suburb of **Miskolc-Tapolca,** *Juno* (tel. 64–133) and *Park* (tel. 60–811), both (M), and comfortable. Guest houses, campsites and paying-guest accommodations.

Restaurants. *Alabárdos* and *Bükk* in town center; *Kisvadász* at Tapolca.

Sárospatak. *Bodrog* (M), (tel. 11–744), new. *Borostyán* (M), (tel. 11–611); campsites; paying-guest accommodations.

Szilvásvárad. *Lipicai* (I), (tel. 55–100), simple but comfortable, some private baths; tourist-hostel, campsite, paying-guest accommodations.

Szirák. *Kastély* (M), (tel. 37); late-17th-century castle-hotel; refurbished and decorated to a high standard. All rooms with bath. Riding facilities available.

Tokaj. *Tokaj* (M), (tel. 58), doubles with private bath. First-class international campsite; paying-guest accommodations.

Restaurants. *Rákóczi, Tiszavirág Halászcsárda* (fish), and many snack bars and wine bars. The *Rákóczi Cellar,* which may be visited, contains 20,000 hectoliters (nearly 450,000 gallons) of wine.

THE GREAT PLAIN

Magyar to the Core

The Great Plain, which stretches from Budapest as far as the borders of Romania and Yugoslavia and covers an area of some 51,800 sq. km. (20,000 sq. miles), is what most people think of as the typical Hungarian landscape. Almost completely flat, it is the home of shepherds and their flocks and, above all, of splendid horses and the *csikós,* their riders. The plain has a wild, almost alien, air; its sprawling villages consist mostly of one-story houses, though there are many large farms and up-to-date market gardens. The Plain, which is divided into two almost equal parts by the River Tisza, also contains several of Hungary's most historic cities.

Three main road routes link Budapest with the Great Plain. The first leads east to Szolnok, Debrecen, Nyíregyháza and the Soviet frontierpoint of Záhony; the second southeast to Kecskemét and Szeged; the third, hugging the Danube, south to Kalocsa and Baja.

The most northerly part of the region is known as the Nyírség; it borders on the Soviet and Romanian frontiers and its chief town is Nyíregyháza. This will hardly detain the visitor, who, however, will find a famous medicinal spa, Sóstó, only six km. (four miles) away and easily reached by bus. From an architectural point of view the most interesting place in the district is Nyírbátor, 39 km. (24 miles) east of Nyíregyháza and easily reached by train or bus;

it has a very fine 15th-century Gothic Protestant church; a musical festival is held in the church in July.

Debrecen and the Hortobágy

Forty-eight km. (30 miles) south of Nyíregyháza is Debrecen, one of the largest and historically most important towns of Hungary. It is the economic and cultural center of Eastern Hungary and a town with a character all its own—its inhabitants have called it "the Calvinist Rome" and most of its people are Protestants. Its University has always been famous as a center of learning and its predecessor, the Calvinist College, was founded more than 400 years ago. In its Great Church Hungarian independence from the Habsburgs was proclaimed by Kossuth in 1849. Here, too, in 1944, the anti-Nazi coalition government met, bringing the hope of peace to the war-ravaged country.

Debrecen has been inhabited since the Stone Age. It was already a sizable village by the end of the 12th century and by the 14th century it was a privileged and important market town. After the Reformation it became—and has remained—the stronghold of Hungarian Protestantism.

The street leading from the railway station to the Great Church contains many of Debrecen's most interesting buildings. The Old County Hall was built in 1912 in what is known as the "Hungarian style," with majolica ornaments. In the neo-Classical Town Hall, farther on, Kossuth lived in 1849. The Great Church, which faces a tree-lined square, is the largest Protestant place of worship in Hungary; it was built early in the 19th century in an impressive neo-Classical style. Near it are the original Calvinist College, already referred to, and one of Hungary's best-known hotels, the art nouveau Arany Bika (Golden Bull), whose cuisine is famous. In the northern part of the city lies the Nagyerdő (Great Forest), a large park with thermal establishments and every facility for water sports.

Just over 19 km. (12 miles) south of Debrecen lies Hajdúszoboszló, one of Hungary's oldest and most famous medicinal spas.

Stretching for many miles to the west of Debrecen is the Hortobágy, the most typical and most romantic part of the Great Plain, a grassy *puszta* or prairie covering over 100,000 hectares (250,000 acres). Though much of it has, in recent years, become agricultural land, there is still enough of its unique atmosphere left to attract the foreign visitor. The center of the Hortobágy is where highway 33 crosses the Hortobágy river on a famous nine-arched bridge dating from the beginning of the 19th century. Near it is the Nagycsárda (Great Inn), built in 1699; there are guest rooms, a restaurant and a cafe. "Equestrian Days" are arranged here every summer.

The road (highway 4) from Budapest to Debrecen passes just north of Cegléd and through Szolnok, two towns which are chiefly of importance as road and railway junctions and as the economic centers of important agricultural districts. Cegléd has a neo-Classical Protestant church of some interest. Szolnok lies on the River Tisza and is the geometrical center of the Great Plain. It has several fine old churches, among them the high-Baroque Franciscan church near the river bank. In addition it houses a well-known artists' colony and has good facilities for swimming and other water sports. It is now an important industrial center.

Kecskemét

Both highway 5 and motorway M5 (under construction) lead us southeast from Budapest to Kecskemét, one of the most characteristic of Hungarian towns, with a population of around 100,000; it is an important railway junction and the center of a large and rich agricultural district. Here is one of the most valuable fruit-growing areas in the country; it produces the delicious Hungarian apricots, from which the famous *barack*, the fiery yet smooth apricot-brandy, is made.

The heart of the sprawling town is formed by two vast squares which join each other: Szabadság (Liberty) and Kossuth Squares. In Szabadság Square is a remarkable double Synagogue, recently restored and housing some public collections. A fine, Hungarian-style art nouveau building called the Cifrapalota (Ornamental Palace) stands opposite; today it is the home of the local trade union council. In Kossuth Square is the Town Hall, built in 1893–96 by Ödön Lechner in the Hungarian art nouveau style which he created. There are several interesting churches in Kecskemét, including the Baroque "Old Church" (1772–1805), just north of the Town Hall; the oldest and most important building in Kossuth Square is the Szent Miklós Templom (Church of St. Nicholas), on the south side, originally built in a Gothic style in the 15th century but rebuilt in a Baroque style in the 18th. A little to the west of the town center, in Gáspár András Utca, stands the Magyar Naiv Festők Múzeuma (Museum of Hungarian Naïve Artists). Kecskemét has an artists' colony and was the birthplace of the composer Kodály. An excursion can be made to Kiskőrös, 48 km. (30 miles) to the southwest along road 54; here Sándor Petőfi, one of Hungary's most famous poets and a leading spirit of the 1848 revolution against the Habsburgs, was born. The tiny house—his father was the village butcher—is now a memorial museum. Kiskőrös can also be reached from Kalocsa on the east bank of the Danube.

About 32 km. (20 miles) south of Kecskemét and easily reached by road lies Bugac *puszta*, the center of a large sandy area, which has provided poets and artists with inexhaustible material. It has a famous inn (the Bugac csárda), with excellent food, drink and music, as well as an open-air museum. While much of the region has now been brought under cultivation, the landscape has kept its character. In the summer there are horse shows (the Hungarian version of rodeos) and festivities with gypsy music. There is also good pheasant-shooting in the woods.

Szeged

Szeged is the traditional economic and cultural center of the southern part of the Great Plain. Its great tourist attraction is its open-air festival (July–August each year), but it has many other features to interest the visitor. It was almost completely rebuilt after a great flood in 1879; and constructed on a concentric plan, not unlike that of Pest. There is an inner boulevard, now named after Lenin, and an outer ring, whose sections, named after Rome, Brussels, Paris, London, Moscow and Vienna, recall the international help given in the reconstruction of the city. Avenues connect these two boulevards like the spokes of a wheel.

The heart of the Inner City is the large Széchenyi Square, full of trees and surrounded by imposing buildings, among them the Town Hall and a large hotel, the Tisza, which has a fine concert hall. The most striking building in Szeged is the Votive Church, or Cathedral, a neo-Romanesque edifice built between 1912 and 1929 in fulfillment of a municipal promise made after the great flood. It is one of Hungary's largest churches and has a splendid organ with 12,000 pipes. The church forms the backdrop to the open-air festival, held in Dóm (Cathedral) Square. The Festival started in 1933 and has been held ever since, though with occasional gaps. The stage is huge—502 sq. meters (600 sq. yards)—and the square can hold an audience of 7,000. Outstanding performances are occasionally given of Hungary's great national drama, *The Tragedy of Man,* by Imre Madách. The program contains a rich variety of theatrical pieces, operas and concerts.

Dóm Square is impressive, with arcaded buildings, among them scientific institutes and a theological college. In the center of the Square stands an isolated Romanesque tower, which was formerly part of the 11th-century Dömötör Templom (Church of St. Demetrius). Other interesting sights are the Baroque Greek Orthodox Church, in the Inner City, built between 1743 and 1745, and the so-called Alsóvárosi Templom (Lower City Church), in the southwest part of the town. This was built in the 15th and 16th centuries, but much of it is now in a Baroque style.

Szeged is famous for its paprika, an important ingredient of Hungarian cuisine. It has two universities. Újszeged (New Szeged), on the opposite side of the river, is something of a holiday resort, with every facility for water sports and an open-air theater.

To the northeast of Szeged and near the Romanian border there are several places of interest. One of them, Gyula, has recently developed into a spa of some importance. It has an interesting medieval castle and plays are performed each summer in the castle courtyard.

There is much of this vast central part of the Great Plain that we have not touched on, but a visitor with time to spare—and, if possible, a slight knowledge of Hungarian—will find in many of its small towns things of interest which reflect, perhaps more accurately than anywhere else in Hungary, the genuine life and customs of Hungarian country people.

The East Bank of the Danube

Highway 51 leads due south from Budapest, never far from the east bank of the Danube. Apart from the town of Ráckeve, on the Danube island of Csepel, where there is a museum in the former palace of Prince Eugene of Savoy as well as an interesting Serbian Orthodox church, there is little to detain the traveler until he reaches Kalocsa. This is a town unusually rich in architectural beauty and in memorials of Hungarian cultural history. It was formerly on the Danube, but now, because of a change in the river's course, lies over six km. (four miles) away from it. Kalocsa is rich in charming Baroque buildings. The cathedral, the seat of a Roman Catholic archbishop, was built between 1735 and 1754. The archbishop's palace is another fine Baroque edifice; the archiepiscopal library is one of the most valuable in Hungary, with over 100,000 volumes and many rarities. Kalocsa is famous, too, for its richly colored embroideries, created by its "painting women," examples of whose exquisite work can be seen in a permanent exhibition in the town and can, of course, be bought. Kalocsa can also, though not without inconvenience, be reached by train; the walls of its rail station are covered with examples of this beautiful form of decoration. Kalocsa is, like Szeged, famous for its paprika.

Highway 51 brings us in another 43 km. (27 miles) to the pleasant town of Baja, built on an arm of the Danube. It contains several interesting Baroque churches. Béke (Peace) Square, on the river bank, is lined with fine old houses. A bridge from the square leads to Petőfi Island, where there is a pleasant beach and a large stadium. Baja boasts a considerable artists' colony.

PRACTICAL INFORMATION FOR
THE GREAT PLAIN

TOURIST INFORMATION. The following are the addresses of the local tourist offices. **Baja:** Béke Tér; **Cegléd:** Szabadság Tér; **Debrecen:** next to **Arany Bika** Hotel; **Gyula:** Kossuth Lajos Utca; **Hajdúszoboszló:** in spa quarter; **Hortobágy:** in the village; **Kalocsa:** in town center; **Kecskemét:** Kossuth Tér; **Nyíregyháza:** Dózsa György Út; **Szeged:** Klauzál Tér; **Szolnok:** Kossuth Lajos Utca.

WHEN TO COME. Spring, summer or fall are best, especially as the most interesting events and festivals are held in July and August.

GETTING AROUND. There are good rail connections from Budapest (East and West Stations); local trains and buses complete the network. Otherwise traveling by car gives you the greatest freedom.

HOTELS AND RESTAURANTS

All the hotels listed below have restaurants unless otherwise stated.

Baja. *Sugovica* (M), (tel. 12–988), on Petőfi Island; pool. *Duna* (I), Béke Tér. (tel. 11–765). Campsites.
Restaurant. *Halászcsárda* (fish), on Petőfi Island.

Bugac. Bungalows; paying-guest accommodations.

Cegléd. *Kossuth* (I), (tel. 10–990). Paying-guest accommodations.
Restaurants. *Alföld, Magyar, Zöld Hordó.*

Debrecen. *Arany Bika* (M), (tel. 16–777), a historic hostelry famous for its food. *Főnix* (I), (tel. 13–355). *Debrecen* (I), (tel. 16–550). Campsites and paying-guest accommodations; bungalows in Nagyerdő Park, to the north of town.
Restaurants. *Gambrinus, Hungária,* and *Szabadság* all in town center. *Újvigadó* and several others in Nagyerdő Park.

Gyula. *Park* (I), (tel. 62–622); *Komló* (I), (tel. 61–041), simple. *Aranykereszt Szálló* (I), (tel. 62–057). Motel, tourist-hostel, campsites and paying-guest accommodations.
Restaurant. *Budrió,* Béke Sugárút.

Hajdúszoboszló. *Délibáb* (M), (tel. 60–808). *Gambrinus* (I), (tel. 60–100). Campsites; paying-guest accommodations.
Restaurants. *Alföldi,* Hősök Tere, *Szigeti Halászcsárda* (fish), near the thermal baths.

Hortobágy. *Hortobágy Nagy Csárda* (I), (tel. 69–139); *Csárda Inn* (I), (tel. 69–139), both have double rooms with shower. Tourist-hostel; campsites; good restaurant.

Kalocsa. *Piros Arany* (I), (tel. 200). Paying-guest accommodations.
Restaurant. *Kalocsai Csárda,* István Utca.

Kecskemét. *Aranyhomok* (I), (tel. 20–011). Guest houses; campsites; paying-guest accommodations.
Restaurants. *Hirös,* Rákóczi Utca, *Strand,* Sport Utca, and many others.

Nyírbátor. Paying-guest accommodations.

Nyíregyháza. *Szabolcs* (M), (tel. 12–333). *Kemév* (I), (tel. 10–606). Paying-guest accommodations. (See also under **SÓSTÓ,** a spa six km. (four miles) to the north.)

Ráckeve. *Keve* (M), (tel. 85–147), new and comfortable. Campsites; paying-guest accommodations.

Sóstó. *Krúdy* (M), (tel. 12–424). *Svájci Lak* (I), (tel. 12–424). Tourist-hostel; holiday-village; campsite; paying-guest accommodations.

Szeged. *Hungária* (M), (tel. 21–210), modern, on river bank. *Royal* (M), (tel. 12–911). *Tisza* (M), (tel. 12–466), in town center, older, but comfortable. Several guest houses, bungalows, campsites; paying-guest accommodations.
Restaurants. *Alabárdos,* Oskola Utca. *Hági,* Kelemen Utca, recommended. *Gambrinus Beerhouse,* Deák Utca. *Halászcsárda* (fisherman's inn), on the river bank. *Szeged,* Széchenyi Tér. Many snack bars.

Szolnok. *Pelikán* (M), (tel. 13–356), new and comfortable. *Tisza* (M), (tel. 17–666), older, doubles with bath. *Touring* (M), (tel. 12–928), in the park. Two motels; campsites; paying-guest accommodations.
Restaurants. *Aranylakat,* in the park. *Múzeum,* Kossuth Tér. *Nemzeti,* Ságvári Körút.

WESTERN HUNGARY

Civilized and Mellow

Western Hungary—often known as "Transdanubia" (Dunántúl in Hungarian)—is that part of Hungary south and west of the Danube, stretching to the Czech and Austrian borders in the north and west and to Yugoslavia in the south. It is an undulating country, with several ranges of hills and outposts from the Alps. The part of the region around Lake Balaton we have already described in an earlier chapter.

Western Hungary's climate is rather more humid than that of the rest of the country; most of its surface is covered with farmland, vineyards and orchards. It presents a highly picturesque landscape with many attractions for the tourist.

The Romans called the region Pannonia; for centuries it was a frontier province and it is richer in Roman remains than the rest of Hungary. The towns are mostly old and have highly civilized traditions. Some industrial complexes have recently developed, the most important of them being at Dunaújváros, a large iron and steel town on the west bank of the Danube.

Győr and Pannonhalma

Entering Western Hungary at Hegyeshalom, on the Austrian border, the first important town one reaches is Győr. It lies exactly halfway between Vienna and Budapest and is both an ancient city and a modern industrial community. It was known to the Romans as Arrabona and here they built a fortress on what is now Káptalan (Chapter) Hill, in the heart of the Old Town. Most of the streets below the hill are built in a regular, checkboard pattern, dating from the 16th century, and many of them are extremely picturesque. The most beautiful Baroque church is the Carmelite church (1721–1725) in Köztársaság (Republic) Square, whose eastern side is lined with fine Baroque houses. The Castle district on Káptalan Hill contains Győr's oldest church, the Cathedral, whose foundations are believed to go back to the time of St. Stephen (11th century). It has been frequently rebuilt and is now largely Baroque, though with a neo-Classical facade. In the Héderváry chapel (15th century) is a masterpiece of medieval Hungarian goldsmith's art, the reliquary of King St. Ladislas (1040–1095).

Altogether the streets and squares of the Old Town present one of the most delightful Baroque townscapes of Hungary. They include the Bishop's Castle, opposite the Cathedral, the Diocesan Library and Museum, the house at 4 Alkotmány Street in which Napoleon stayed in 1809 (now a museum) and many other interesting buildings too numerous to mention.

About 21 km. (13 miles) southeast of Győr lies the great Benedictine Abbey of Pannonhalma, which dates back a thousand years. In the Middle Ages it was immensely powerful and, though, of course, it no longer exerts any political influence, it still pursues its tasks of religion and learning and has a large and important grammar school.

The present abbey was rebuilt in Baroque style on 13th-century foundations. Its cloisters are the sole surviving monument of monastic architecture of the Árpád dynasty. The abbey church is the only early Gothic church in Hungary, but there have been many later additions, including a 52-meter (165-ft.) high tower in a classical style built early in the 19th century. The library, which contains 300,000 volumes, is one of the most important in Hungary. The archives contain priceless 11th- and 12th-century documents, including the foundation deed of the abbey at Tihany, on Lake Balaton, dating from 1055 and the first Hungarian document to contain a large number of Hungarian words inserted into its Latin text. The abbey also contains a superb collection of ecclesiastical plate and vestments.

Tata and Tatabánya

Continuing eastwards from Győr or towards Budapest you reach Tata, another of Hungary's interesting old towns; it is also a spa and well-known equestrian center. On the shores of the large lake, which is in the middle of the town, stands the Castle, medieval in origin but rebuilt at the end of the last century. It contains a museum of local history. Most of the town is Baroque, designed by the

architect Jakab Fellner on the instructions of Count József Esterházy between 1751 and 1787. The Hungarian Olympic training
camp is at Tata, which is one of the country's leading sports centers. At Remeteségpuszta nearby there are opportunities for riding.

At Bábolna, on a minor road between Győr and Tata, is one of
Hungary's chief horse-breeding centers, with a museum.

Tatabánya, a few miles further on, is a fast-growing industrial
town, with important coal mines, factories and power-stations, but
little to detain the tourist. From here it is 56 km. (35 miles) along
the M1 motorway to Budapest.

Sopron, Fertőd and the Esterházy Palace

Sopron lies on the Austrian frontier, between Lake Fertő (in
German *Neusiedlersee*) and the Sopron Hills and is one of the most
picturesque towns in Hungary. It has many historical and cultural
monuments and it enjoys a sub-alpine climate—cooler than the sul-
try lowlands in summer and sheltered by its hills from the harsh
western winds in winter.

The chief sights of Sopron, mostly Medieval and Baroque, are
to be found in the horseshoe-shaped inner town, which was formerly enclosed by the city walls. Széchenyi Square—not far from the
main rail station—links the two ends of the boulevard that follows
the horseshoe line of the city. The former Dominican church, on
the south side of the square, is a fine example of Baroque
(1719–1725). Petőfi Square lies to the west and two curving streets
lead from this square to Lenin Boulevard, a long, busy shopping
street and promenade, built on the site of a former moat. On the
odd-numbered side of the boulevard are a whole row of interesting
Baroque, Rococo and Classical houses. Near the Előkapu (Outer
Gate), leading into the inner town, stands the Baroque St. Mary
Column (1745).

Further on along the boulevard we find several outstanding
buildings; the Patika-ház (no. 29) has been the home of the Arany
Sas (Golden Eagle) pharmacy since 1724; no. 55 was formerly the
Fehér Ló (White Horse) Inn, where Haydn often stayed and where
Johann Strauss composed part of his *One Night in Venice.* The Előkapu (referred to above) is a short street, with medieval houses,
leading to the spacious Fő Tér (Main Square) through a passage
under the 56-meter (180-ft.) high Várostorony (City Tower). The
tower—the symbol of the city—was begun not later than the 12th
or 13th century, though it has clearly-marked Romanesque, Renaissance and Baroque additions.

The square contains many fine buildings, varying from Gothic,
through Baroque, to the late 19th-century Town Hall. The Benedictine church was built between 1280 and 1300; its 43-meter (144-
ft.) high steeple dates from the 14th century. In the interesting
Gothic interior five national assemblies were held between 1553
and 1681 and three kings and queens were crowned. The Storno

house, near the City Tower, is Sopron's most beautiful Baroque building; still in private ownership, it houses a fine collection of furniture, porcelain and paintings. The 1701 Baroque statue of the Trinity in the middle of the Square is the oldest such monument in Hungary. The Baroque Fabricius House, in the same square, contains some of the exhibits of the Ferenc Liszt Museum, the main building of which is situated just west of the inner town, in Május 1. (May 1st) Square.

Templom (Church) Street leads to the south. Here the former Esterházy Palace, part medieval, part Baroque, contains a Mining Museum. Most of the other houses in this street are officially-protected Gothic or Baroque monuments. Új (New) Street, to the east, in spite of its name one of Sopron's oldest streets, contains several interesting buildings, including a medieval synagogue, unique in Hungary, now a religious museum. The former Erdődy Palace, in Szent György (St. George) Street, close by, is the finest Rococo building in Sopron. Almost all of the narrow and picturesque streets of the inner town and those just outside it offer views of historic and picturesque buildings.

The most interesting excursion from Sopron is to Fertőd, 17 miles (27 km.) to the southeast, where the largest and most splendid Baroque palace in Hungary, the Esterházy Palace, stands. It is easily reached by bus from Sopron; it also lies only a short distance north of one of the main roads between Vienna and Budapest—and so is easily reached by motorists. The palace was built between 1760 and 1770 by Prince Miklós (Nicholas) Esterházy. Though badly damaged in World War II, it has been painstakingly and beautifully restored. It attracts over 200,000 visitors annually, partly because of the celebrated concerts held here each year and also because of the Haydn Memorial Museum. Haydn was the court conductor of the great Esterházy family from 1761 till 1790. The palace contains 126 rooms; it is horseshoe-shaped and is surrounded by splendid gardens. In the magnificent white and gold ballroom Haydn conducted the first performance of his "Farewell Symphony." The house in which Haydn lived and a contemporary Baroque inn are also fine buildings. One wing of the palace is now a simple "country-house hotel."

Another worthwhile trip is to Nagycenk, 13 km. (eight miles) southeast of Sopron. Here is the former home of the Széchenyi family, where the great Hungarian statesman, Count István Széchenyi, lived for many years and is buried. The beautiful Baroque mansion is now the Széchenyi Memorial Museum. There is also a toy railway, with a steam engine and signal equipment that are 100 years old.

Szombathely and Kőszeg

Another interesting town, also not far from the Austrian border, is Szombathely. It was the Roman Savaria and has for centuries been an important economic center. It has several sights which will appeal to the tourist. Two important squares lie in the town center—Köztársaság (Republic) Square and Berzsenyi Square. Köztársaság Square, formerly the marketplace, is still the business center of the city. In Berzsenyi Square are the Baroque cathedral and Bishops' Palace, which, with adjoining buildings, form a harmonious whole. To the south lie the remains of the Temple of Isis, which are believed to date from the 2nd century A.D. Here devotees of a cult which originated in Egypt used to worship. The Savaria Festival takes place in the grounds each summer.

Several interesting excursions can easily be made from Szombathely. Kőszeg, 16 km. (ten miles) to the north, is reached by frequent trains in about half an hour. It is one of Hungary's most fascinating small towns. It lies higher than any other town in the country (270 meters/855 ft. above sea-level), among the eastern outcrops of the Alps, and is very rich in medieval monuments; indeed, its appearance can have changed little since the Middle Ages. It is, too, important historically; the stand of a few hundred Hungarian troops here in 1532 forced the Turkish army of almost 200,000 to abandon their attempt to capture Vienna. A gate in Jurisich Square (Jurisich was the Hungarian commander) was erected in 1932 to commemorate the historic event. The square leads to the heart of the old town, in which medieval churches, houses and public buildings alike preserve their ancient appearance. The Castle contains an interesting museum.

Ják, 11 km. (seven miles) south of Szombathely, has the finest Romanesque church in Hungary, dating from the period of the Árpád Dynasty, with two fine towers, crowned with spires. The outside of the church, particularly the west door, is profusely ornamented with carvings. It is reached by road; there is a regular bus service.

Sárvár and Bük

Two other places worth a visit from Szombathely are Sárvár and Bük. Sárvár lies 27 km. (17 miles) east of Szombathely on the left bank of the Rába. Its castle, first mentioned in the 12th century, became an important cultural center during the Reformation. Its halls contain a memorial exhibition devoted to Sebestyén Tinódi Lantos (1505–1556), a famous wandering minstrel, much of whose work has survived. The first book printed in Hungary in the Hungarian language, a Latin-Hungarian grammar, was printed here in 1539, as was the first Hungarian translation of the New Testament (1541). The little town's streets are lined with old houses and the castle gardens have many rare trees. Sárvár has now become a spa of some importance.

Bük (also known as Bükfürdő; "fürdő" means "spa" or "bath") is 32 km. (20 miles) northeast of Szombathely. It too has valuable alkaline waters, mainly used for the treatment of locomotor and

gynecological diseases. One of the picturesque "country-house hotels" is located here—a Baroque building, once the home of the
Szapáry family.

There are frequent trains from Szombathely to both Sárvár and
Bük.

Veszprém and the Bakony Hills

Veszprém is not only a picturesque center of cultural and economic life, but also unique in Hungary in that it is built on five
hills and in the intervening valleys. Its traffic center is Szabadság
(Liberty) Square, on which is situated the Baroque Town Hall.

The most interesting quarter of the town lies to the north and
is approached along Rákóczi Road; this ends in Vöröshadsereg
(Red Army) Square, at the top of the Várhegy (Castle Hill). Here
is the southern entrance to the Castle, which rises on a dolomite
rock 30 meters (100 ft.) above its surroundings. The Hősi kapu
(Heroes' Gate), at the entrance to the Castle, contains the Castle
Museum. On the left a short cul-de-sac leads to the Tűztorony
(Fire Tower), which is partly medieval and partly Baroque; its gallery offers a fine panorama of the town and its environs. Continuing
along Tolbuhin Street we pass the fine Baroque Bishop's Palace;
the 13th-century Gizella chapel adjoining it is one of Hungary's
most famous early Gothic buildings, with contemporary murals.

The road ends in a spacious square where, on the left, stands St.
Michael's Cathedral, one of the most precious architectural features of Veszprém. The city has been an episcopal see since the
time of King St. Stephen and the cathedral was begun in the 11th
century in a Romanesque style; in the 14th century Gothic details
were added. It was remodeled along Baroque lines in the 18th century, after destruction by the Turks, while in the 20th century it
was recast in a neo-Romanesque style. Its Baroque and Classical
altars are exceedingly fine and there is a large collection of plate
and vestments in the sacristy. The new town of Veszprém is being
developed in and around Rákóczi Square, east of the traditional
center, while the university district lies to the south of the town.

The Bakony lies to the west of Veszprém, north of Lake Balaton.
It is a hilly and forested area and one of the most attractive regions
of Hungary. Its ruined castles recall the age of chivalry, its ancient
cultural centers confirm long-established traditions, while new
mines and industrial plants have much improved the region's standard of living. Communications are fairly good, both by rail and
road.

About 16 km. (ten miles) west of Veszprém lies Herend, the
Hungarian Sèvres or Nymphenburg. The porcelain works were
founded in the 19th century and its products are world famous.
A museum showing some of the best examples of Herend work
is open to the public. Twenty-two km. (14 miles) to the north of
Veszprém lies Zirc, an important tourist center with many historic

buildings. In Rákóczi Square there is a large group of buildings of which the former abbey and church of the Cistercians (founded in 1182) form part. The large, ornate Baroque church was built between 1739 and 1753; its interior is particularly rich, with murals by Maulbertsch. The former abbey is now a library and museum. There are many attractive small resorts around Zirc. Bakonybél, 17 km. (some ten miles) to the west, is the site of the first Benedictine monastery in Hungary.

Pápa, still further west, is an important town lying on the railway to Pannonhalma and Győr. It is the economic and cultural center of the western Bakony. The former Esterházy Castle, built between 1773 and 1782, lies on the northern side of Szabadság (Liberty) Square. The large Baroque parish church (1774–1783) was built by Jakab Fellner and is decorated with murals by Maulbertsch. A Protestant college was established here in 1531 and two of Hungary's greatest 19th-century writers, Petőfi and Jókai, were students here.

Székesfehérvár

Székesfehérvár lies some 40 km. (25 miles) east of Veszprém and is one of the most interesting and important provincial towns of Hungary; it is also one of the country's most important traffic junctions. Known to the Romans as Herculia, its neo-Latin name of Alba Regia was bestowed on it during the Middle Ages. Under King Stephen it was already an important place and it was he who built its first cathedral and royal palace. Although the royal capital was established at Esztergom, and later transferred to Óbuda and then to Buda, Székesfehérvár long preserved its royal links—until 1527 Hungarian kings were crowned here and many were buried here. The town has played an important role throughout Hungarian history and latterly it has become a very busy industrial center.

Szabadság (Liberty) Square is the hub of the city and almost all the sights lie close by. In the square itself lies the Town Hall, a Baroque building, with beautiful gates at its eastern end, and the Bishop's Palace begun in 1790 in an Empire and Biedermeyer style. To the south of the square, in Arany János Street, stands the Baroque Cathedral, built in 1758–78 on the site of an earlier medieval church. King Bela III, who ruled from 1174 to 1196, and his consort were buried in the crypt. At the eastern end of Szabadság Square is the Garden of Ruins (Romkert) on the site of the former cathedral and royal palace, both of which have been extensively excavated. There are many fine Baroque buildings all over the old town, and pleasant cafes and restaurants, together with shady gardens, so that a stroll will prove both interesting and agreeable.

Only a few miles away and just south of the road from Székesfehérvár to Lake Balaton lie Tác and the recently-excavated ruins of the Roman city of Gorsium. A restaurant and cafe have been opened here.

Not far to the east of Székesfehérvár lies Lake Velence, with a number of popular summer resorts; part of the lake is a protected haunt of water birds. Still further to the east, on the way to Budapest, lies Martonvásár, with the picturesque Brunswick Palace, built in 1773–75 but rebuilt in an "English" Gothic style a century later. Beethoven often stayed here and Beethoven Memorial Concerts are held each year in June and July.

Pécs and Southwest Hungary

Southwest Hungary, the district lying south of Lake Balaton, is a smiling, fertile region. Its climate is much milder than elsewhere in Hungary and in the extreme south of the region there are some fair-sized hills. The chief city of the entire region is Pécs, the third-largest provincial town in Hungary. It was the Roman Sopianae, the capital of southern Pannonia, and here several Roman commercial and military roads met. Its great four-towered cathedral rests on Roman foundations. Pécs has always been a prosperous town and was an important staging-post for German and Italian merchants on their way to Byzantium. Hungary's first university was founded here in 1367. During the 143 years of Turkish rule (1543–1686), Pécs acquired a new architectural image, some of which remains to this day.

The center of the town is Széchenyi Square. This contains, among many other old buildings, one dating from the time of the Turkish occupation; the Gazi Kassim Pasha mosque, the largest Turkish monument in Hungary, is now a parish church. Built in the 16th century, it still has its mihrab, the Muslim prayer-niche facing Mecca. Along Janus Pannonius Street, to the northwest, we reach the ecclesiastical center of the city, Dóm (Cathedral) Square, itself a fine piece of architectural planning. The entire northern side of the square is taken up by the Cathedral, one of the most splendid medieval monuments in Hungary. It was begun by King Stephen, but has been rebuilt and remodeled several times. Of its four great, spire-capped towers, two date from the 11th and two from the 12th century. Both externally and internally, the cathedral is impressive and beautiful. On the west side of the square is the Bishop's Palace, whose garden facade is perhaps the finest Baroque monument in Pécs. Nearby there are some early Christian catacombs. Excavations at the southern end of the square are now open to visitors. They have brought to light some remarkable wall paintings in the catacombs, now carefully preserved behind glass.

At Janus Pannonia Utca 11 is the Csontváry Museum, which houses the chief works of the artist Tivadar Csontváry Kosztka, the importance of whose neo-surrealist *oeuvre* was not fully recognized until 50 years after his death in 1919.

Other buildings of note in the city include several Turkish monuments. One is the Jakovali Hassan mosque, in Rákóczi Street, southwest of the town center, built late in the 16th century; this is the only Turkish building in Hungary to have survived intact and it still has its minaret. It is now a museum. Another is the *türbe* (tomb) of Idris Baba, northwest of the inner city; there are also many fine Baroque churches and houses in and around Széchenyi Square.

Pécs is famous for the Zsolnay porcelain produced here since 1851. The Zsolnay Museum, in Káptalan (Chapter) Street, which links the Cathedral Square with the northern part of the town center and which is lined with fine old houses, each an "ancient monument," contains valuable examples of Zsolnay ware. The Vasarely Museum, in the same street, contains the works presented by the famous artist to his home town. Pécs is also a university city and is rapidly developing into an important industrial town.

Two towns well worth visiting from Pécs are Szigetvár and Siklós, both of which have interesting medieval castles. The castle at Szigetvár played an important role in the fight against the Turkish invaders of Hungary in 1566, when a handful of soldiers held out against the army of Sultan Soliman II. There is a Turkish mosque in the castle courtyard. At Siklós, about 32 km. (20 miles) due south of Pécs, the castle has been continuously inhabited since the Middle Ages and now houses a comfortable hotel. The town lies in the center of a rich wine-producing district at the foot of the Villany Hills.

The West Bank of the Danube

There remains to be mentioned the country along the west bank of the Danube. Mohács, 40 km. (25 miles) to the east of Pécs, lies on the river and is famous above all for the disastrous battle fought there in 1526, in which the defending Hungarians were routed by the Turkish army of Sultan Soliman II. It contains a number of pleasant Baroque churches, but nothing of special interest. The town is also noted for its Carnival procession, when many of the participants wear horror masks. It has a nudist camp. Szekszárd, 43 km. (27 miles) further north, lies some miles to the west of the present course of the Danube. The former County Hall, built in 1780 on the site of a Benedictine abbey, and a late Baroque Roman Catholic church are its chief sights. Liszt spent much of his time here and gave several concerts. Szekszárd is the center of notable vineyards, famous from Roman times; and the Gemenc forest nearby is a well-known game reserve.

Finally we must mention Dunaújváros, almost exactly halfway between Szekszárd and Budapest. It is Hungary's greatest purely industrial city. Until the Fifties, it was no more than a small village. It has no buildings of historical importance, but it will interest those—and they amount to over 100,000 visitors a year—who wish to see how a small country has, in not much over 30 years, transformed a sleepy country hamlet into an industrial complex, with vast iron and steel works. A museum illustrates the town's growth.

PRACTICAL INFORMATION FOR
WESTERN HUNGARY

TOURIST INFORMATION. The following are the addresses of the local tourist offices. **Bük:** Termál Körút 43; **Dunaújváros:** Korányi Utca; **Fertőd:** in the Castle; **Győr:** next to Hotel Rába, in town center; **Ják:** opposite the church; **Kőszeg:** Várkör; **Mohács:** Tolbuhin Utca; **Pannonhalma:** close to the Abbey; **Pápa:** Fő Tér 12; **Pécs:** Széchenyi Tér; **Sárvár:** Várkerület 33; **Siklós:** in village center; **Sopron:** Lenin Körút, near Pannonia Hotel; **Székesfehérvár:** Március 15. Utca and Ady Endre Utca, both just north of town center; also opposite Alba Regia Hotel; **Szekszárd:** Széchenyi Tér; **Szigetvár:** Zrínyi Tér; **Szombathely:** Mártírok Tere and Köztársaság Tér; **Tata:** Ady Endre Utca; **Veszprém:** Münnich Ferenc Tér.

WHEN TO COME. Spring, summer and fall are all delightful times to visit western Hungary. Most of the more interesting festivals and popular events are held in July and August.

GETTING AROUND. There are good rail connections from Budapest (South and East Stations). Traveling from Vienna it is necessary to change trains at the frontier station Hegyeshalom. Local trains and buses are adequate. Of course, a car provides you with the greatest freedom.

HOTELS AND RESTAURANTS

All the hotels listed below have restaurants unless otherwise stated.

Bük. *Thermál* (E), (tel. 13–366), modern and comfortable spa hotel. *Bük* (M), (tel. 13–363). *Kastély* (I), (tel. 205), Baroque "country-house hotel" with period furniture, a number of valuable pictures, and fine plasterwork in its great hall; some doubles have bath. Campsite; paying-guest accommodations.

Dunaújváros. *Arany Csillag* (M), (tel. 18–045). Guest house; campsite; paying-guest accommodations.
Restaurants. *Dunagyöngye, Kohász.*

Fertőd. *Kastély* (tel. 45–971); simple "country-house hotel." No private baths. Guest house, tourist hostel, paying-guest accommodations.
Restaurant. *Haydn,* in the village, recommended.

Győr. *Rába* (M), (tel. 15–533). Large, modern hotel. Guest houses, campsite, paying-guest accommodations.
Restaurants. *Hungária,* Lenin Út 23, *Vaskakas,* Köztársaság Tér 3, and many others.

Kőszeg. *Írottkő* (M), (tel. 333); *Expressz-Panoráma* (I), (tel. 280), on hills west of town; *Strucc* (I), (tel. 7281), historic hostelry dating from the

17th century. Two tourist hostels, one in the ancient castle, the other outside the town; paying-guest accommodations; snack bar in castle.

Mohács. *Csele* (M), (tel. 10–825). *Korona* (I), (tel. 10–541). Paying-guest accommodations.
Restaurants. *Béke,* in the town; *Halászcsárda* (fisherman's inn on the island).

Pápa. *Platán* (M), (tel. 24–688). Paying-guest accommodations.
Restaurant. *Béke,* Fő Tér 27.

Pécs. *Nádor* (E), (tel. 10–779), famous old house in the main square. *Főnix* (M), (tel. 11–680). Well placed near the town's main square. *Hunyor* (M), (tel. 15–677), on hills above town with lovely view; serves only breakfast but there is a restaurant close by. *Pannonia* (M), (tel. 13–322), modern, in town. Comfortable. *Fenyves* (I), (tel. 15–996), above town. Guest houses, tourist hostel, campsite; paying-guest accommodations.
Restaurants. *Elefántos Ház,* praised; *Sopiana, Minaret,* in town center; *Vadásztanya,* game specialties, in hills above town.
  Kastély (M), (tel. 12–176) at Üszögpuszta, just outside the city. This, the former Batthyány castle, is now a "country-house hotel" with period furniture; double rooms have up-to-date bathrooms. Tennis and horseriding.

Sárvár. *Thermál* (E), (tel. 16–088), modern and comfortable spa hotel. *Minihotel* (I), (tel. 228); campsite, paying-guest accommodations.

Siklós. *Tenkes* (M–I), (tel. 61), in the medieval castle, some rooms with bath. Guest house, tourist-hostel; paying-guest accommodations.

Sopron. *Lővér* (M), (tel. 11–061), pleasant hotel in the wooded southern outskirts. *Palatinus* (M), (tel. 11–395), in charming town house. *Pannonia* (M), (tel. 12–180), in town center. *Sopron* (M), (tel. 14–254). Outside town, fine views, swimming pool. Several guest houses, tourist-hostels and bungalows; campsites; paying-guest accommodations.
Restaurants. *Cézár, Deák, Gambrinus,* all in town center; *Alpesi,* on hills southwest of the town. Many wine bars.

Székesfehérvár. *Alba Regia* (M), (tel. 13–484), modern and comfortable. *Velence* (I), (tel. 11–262). Old-fashioned, but with some private baths. Guest house, tourist-hostel; campsite; paying-guest accommodations.
Restaurants. *Kiskulacs; Ösféhervár,* in town center, good.

Szekszárd. *Gemenc* (M), (tel. 11–722). *Garay* (I), (tel. 12–177). Guest house; campsite; paying-guest accommodations.
Restaurants. *Halászcsárda* (fish-restaurant), *Kispipa, Szász* (beer hall).

Szigetvár. *Oroszlán* (M), (tel. 284). Tourist-hostel in the castle; paying-guest accommodations.

Szombathely. *Claudius* (E), (tel. 13–760), in park, recommended. *Isis* (M), (tel. 14–990). *Savaria* (M), (tel. 11–440), in Martírok Tere, is an art nouveau masterpiece, recently completely restored both inside and out. *Tourist* (I), (tel. 14–168), in the town. Tourist-hostel; paying-guest accommodations.

Restaurants. *Halászcsárda* (fish-restaurant), *Pannonia,* both in town center; *Tó, Pásztorok,* near lake outside town.

Tata. *Diana* (M), and *Dianatouring* (I), both (tel. 80–388), at Remeteségpuszta, five km. (three miles) out of town, are parts of an old castle converted into a hotel and near the State Riding School, with excellent opportunities for horseriding.

Malom (tel. 81–530), *Kristály* (tel. 80–577) and *Pálma* (tel. 80–577), all (I), are all in the town. Several guest houses, campsites, paying-guest accommodations.

Restaurants. *Aranyponty, Jázmin, Vár, Zsigmond* (wine bar).

Veszprém. *Veszprém* (M), (tel. 12–345), modern and comfortable. Bungalows; paying-guest accommodations; tourist-hostel for students at the University hall of residence during the summer vacation.

Restaurants. *Halle söröző* (beer hall), *Malom* (wine bar), *Vadásztanya.*

Zirc. *Bakony* (I), (tel. 168), simple. Tourist-hostel; paying-guest accommodations.

TOURIST VOCABULARY

Hungarian is very different from the languages of the West and at first
sight looks forbiddingly difficult. It has many double consonants and accented vowels and it is not easy to represent its pronunciation accurately
in a way easily understandable by the ordinary traveler. We have listed
below what we consider to be the most important words and phrases for
the visitor and we have tried to help him (or her) to pronounce them.

There are three important 'keys' to the imitated pronunciation we have
used. 1 *Every* word is strongly accented on the *first* syllable and, to draw
attention to this, we have *italicized* this syllable in the imitated pronunciation. 2 The letter *"o"* in the imitated pronunciation is pronounced like
the short English "o" in the word "on"; the letters *"oh"* represent the longer sound of "o," as in the English word "home". 3 The sign *"u [r]"* represents roughly the *vowel* sound in the English word "hurt", but *the "r" is
not pronounced.*

USEFUL EXPRESSIONS

Hello, how do you do	Jó napot? (*yoh* noppoht?)
How are you?	Hogy van? (hohdge von?)
Good morning	Jó reggelt (*yoh* reg-gelt)
Good evening	Jó estét (*yoh* esh-teht)
Goodnight	Jó éjszakát (*yoh* eysokaht)
Goodbye	Viszontlátásra (*vis*sohnt-lahtahshro)
Please	Kérem [szépen] (*keh*rem [*seh*pen])
Thank you	Köszönöm (*ku*[r]su[r]nu[r]m)
Thank you very much	Köszönöm szépen (*ku*[r]su[r]nu[r]m *seh*pen)
Yes	Igen (*i*gen)
No	Nem (nem)
You're welcome, don't mention it	Nincs mit; szívesen (ninch mit; *see*veshen)
Excuse me	Bocsánat (*boh*chahnot)
Come in!	Szabad! (*sob*od!)
I'm sorry	Sajnálom (*shahee*-nahlohm)
My name is . . .	. . . vagyok (. . . *voj*ohk)
Do you speak English?	Beszél angolul? (*bess*ehl *ong*-gohlul?)
I don't speak Hungarian	Nem tudok magyarul (nem *too*dohk *mo*jorool)
I don't understand	Nem értem (nem *ehr*tem)
Please speak slowly	Kérem beszéljen lassan (*keh*rem *bess*-ehyen *losh*-shon)
Please write it down	Kérem, írja le ezt (*keh*rem, *eer*-yo lay ezt)
Where is . . . ?	Hol van . . . ? (hohl von . . . ?)

What is this place called?	Hogy hívják ezt a helyet? (hodge *heev*yahk ezt o *hey*et?)
Please show me	Megmutatná nekem (*meg*moototnah nekem)
I would like . . .	Szeretnék . . . (*serret*nehk . . .)
How much does it cost?	Mennyibe kerül? (*meny*ibe *ker*ewl?)

SIGNS

Entrance	Bejárat (*be*yahrot)
Exit	Kijárat (*kee*yahrot)
emergency exit	vészkijárat (*vehss*-keeyahrot)
Toilet, lavatory	Toalet, W.C. (*twah*let; *veh*-tseh)
men; gentlemen	férfiak; urak (*fehr*fiok; *oor*ok)
women; ladies	nők; hőlgyek (nu[r]k; *hu*[r]*l*jek)
vacant	szabad (*sob*od)
occupied	foglalt (*foh*glolt)
Hot	Meleg (*mel*leg)
Cold	Hideg (*hidd*eg)
No smoking	Dohányozni tilos (*doh*ahnyozni *till*osh)
No admittance	Tilos a bemenet; nem bejárat (*till*osh o *bemm*enet; nem *bay*ahrot)
Stop	Stop (stohp)
Danger	Veszély (*vess*ay)
Closed	Zárva (*zahr*vo)
Full, no vacancy	Megtelt (*megg*-telt)
Information	Információ (*in*fohrmahtsioh)
Bus stop	Autóbusz megálló (*ow*tohboos *meg*ahl-loh)
Taxi stand	Taxi-állomás (*tok*si-*ahl*-lohmahsh)
Pedestrians	Gyalogjárók (*joll*ohg-yahrohk)

ARRIVAL

Passport check	Útlevélellenőrzes (*oot*levehl-*ell*enu[r]rzehsh)
Your passport, please	Kérem az útlevelét (*keh*rem oz *oot*leveleht)
I am with the group	A csoporttal vagyok (o *chohp*pohrt-tol *voj*ohk)
Customs	Vám (vahm)
anything to declare?	van elvámolni valója? (von *el*vahmohlni *vol*ohyo?)
nothing (to declare)	semmi nincs (*shemm*i ninch)
Baggage	Poggyász (*pohj*-jahss)
Baggage ticket	Poggyászjegy (*pohj*-jahss-yedge)

Transportation

to the bus	az autóbuszhoz (oz *ow*tohbooss-hohz)
to a taxi	egy taxihoz (edge *tok*si-hohz)
to the hotel . . . , please	Kérem, a . . . szállóhoz (*keh*rem, o . . . *sahl*-loh-hohz)

MONEY

Money	Pénz (paynz)
The currency exchange office	A pénzváltás (o *paynz*vahltahsh)
Can you change this?	Fel tudya ezt váltani? (fel *tood*-yo ezt *vahl*toni?)
May I pay . . .	Fizethetek . . . (*fizet*-hetek . . .)
with a travelers' check?	csekkel? (*check*-kel?)
with this credit card?	evvel a kreditkártyával? (*ev*vel o *kred*itkahrtyahvol?)
I would like to exchange some travelers' checks	Szeretnék beváltani néhány csekket (*serr*etnayk *be*vahltoni *nay*-hahn *check*-ket)

THE HOTEL

A hotel	Egy szálló (edge *sahl*-loh)
I have a reservation	Foglaltam egy szobát (*fohg*lahltom edge *soh*baht)
A room with bath	Szoba fürdőszobával (*fewr*du[r]-*soh*bahvol)
a shower	egy zuhany (edge *zoo*-hon)
hot running water	meleg víz (*mell*eg veez)
What floor is it on?	Melyik emeleten van? (*may*-ik *emm*eleten von?)
ground floor	földszint (*fu*[r]*ld*-sint)
second floor	első emelet (*el*-shu[r] *emm*elet)
The elevator	A lift (o lift)
Have the baggage sent up, please	Kérem a poggyászt felküldeni (*keh*rem o *pohj*-jahst *fel*-kewldeni)
The key to number . . . , please	Kérem a kulcsot a . . . es szobához (*keh*rem a *kool*choht o . . . esh *soh*bah-hohz)
Please call me at seven o'clock	Kérem hétkor felkelteni (*keh*rem *hayt*-kohr *fel*-keltenee)
Have the baggage brought down, please	Kérem a poggyászt lehozni (*keh*rem a *pohj*-jahst *leh*-hoznee)
The bill	A számla (o *sahm*-lo)
A tip	Egy borravaló (edge *bohr*-ro-voloh)

THE RESTAURANT

The restaurant	A vendéglő, az étterem (o *vend*ehglu[r], oz *eht*-terem)
Café	Kávéház, eszpresszó (*kah*vayhahz, *e*spressoh)
Menu	Étlap (*ayt*-lop)
Waiter!	Pincér! (*pin*-tsair)
Waitress!	Pincérnő! (*pin*-tsairnu[r]!)

(Both are more likely to respond to the request Kérem—*keh*rem = Please!)

I would like to order this	Kérem ezt (*keh*rem ezt)
Some more . . . , please	Még néhány . . . , kérem (Mehg *nay*-hahn . . . , *keh*rem)
Enough	Elég (*ell*ehg)
The check, please	A számlát kérem; fizetek (o *sahm*laht *keh*rem; *fi*zetek)
Breakfast	Reggeli (*reg*-gellee)
Lunch	Ebéd (*eb*-ehd)
Dinner	Vacsora (*votch*-ohro)
Bread	Kenyér (*ken*-yehr)
Butter	Vaj (voy)
Jam	Lekvár (*lek*vahr)
Salt	Só (shoh)
Pepper	Bors, paprika (bohrsh, *pop*riko)
Mustard	Mustár (*moosh*tahr)
Sauce, gravy	Mártás (*mah*rtahsh)
Vinegar	Ecet (*et*set)
Oil	Olaj (*ohl*oy)
A bottle	Egy üveg (edge *ew*veg)
Wine	Bor (bohr)
red, white wine	vörös, fehér bor (*vu*[r]ru [r]sh, *f*ehehr bohr)
Beer	Sör (shu[r]r)
Spirits (apricot brandy)	Barackpálinka (*bo*rotsk-*pah*lingko)
Water	Víz (veez)
Mineral water	Kristályvíz, Ásványvíz (*krish*tahee veez, *ahsh*-vahn veez)
Milk	Tej (tay)
Coffee	Kávé (*kah*vay)
Tea with lemon	Tea citrommal (*tay*-o *tsit*rohmmol)
Sugar	Cukor (*tsoo*kohr)
Lemonade	Limonádé (*lim*ohnahday)
(Fruit) juice	(Gyümölcs) lé (*jew*-mu(r)lch) lay

MAIL

A letter	Egy levél (edge *lev*ehl)

An envelope	Egy boríték (edge *boh*reetehk)
A postcard	Egy levelező lap (edge *lev*elezu[r] lop)
A mailbox	Egy postaláda (edge *pohsh*to-lahdo)
The post office	A postahivatal (o *pohsh*tohivotol)
A stamp	Egy bélyeg (edge *bay*-yeg)
By airmail	Légi postával (*lay*gi *pohsh*tahvol)
How much does it cost to send a letter, a postcard, airmail to the United States, Great Britain, Canada?	Mennyibe kerül egy levelet, egy levelező lapot, légi postával az Egyesült Államokba, Angliába, Kanadába küldeni? (*men*-nyibeh *ker*ewl edge *lev*elet, edge *lev*elezu[r] lopoht, *lay*gi *pohsh*tahvol oz *Edge*-eshewlt *Ahl*-lomohkbo, *Ong*-gliahbo, *Kon*odahbo *kewl*deni?)
to send a telegram, cable?	Egy táviratot küldeni? (edge *tah*virotoht *kewl*deni?)

LOCATIONS

. . . Street	. . . Utca (. . . *oot*so)
. . . Avenue	. . . Út (. . . ooht)
. . . Square	. . . Tér (. . . tayr)
The airport	A repülőtér (o *rep*ewlu[r]-tayr)
A bank	Egy bank (edge bongk)
The beach	A strand (o shtrond)
The bridge	A híd (o heed)
The castle	A kastély (o *kosh*-tay), a vár (o vahr)
The cathedral	A székesegyház (o *say*kesh-edgehahz)
The church	A templom (o *temp*lohm)
The garden	A kert (o kairt)
The hospital	A kórház (o *kohr*-hahz)
The movies, cinema a movie	A mozi (o *mohz*i) Egy film (edge film)
The museum	A múzeum (o *moo*-zayoom)
A nightclub	Egy mulatóhely (edge *moo*lotoh-hay)
The palace	A palota (o *poll*ohto)
The park	A park (o porrk)
The post office	A postahivatal (o *pohsh*tohivotol)
The restaurant	A vendéglő, az étterem (o *ven*dehglu[r], oz *eht*-terem)
The station	A pályaudvar, a vasúti állomás (o *pah*-yo-oodvor, o *vosh*ooti *ahl*-lomahsh)
The theater a play	A színház (o *seen*-hahz) Egy színdarab (edge *seen*-dorob)
Travel bureau (IBUSZ)	IBUSZ (the official travel agency) (*ib*booss)

in general   Utazási iroda (ootozahshi
                                        eerohdo)
The university   Az egyetem (oz edge-etem)

TRAVEL

Arrival   Érkezés (ehr-kezehsh)
Departure   Indulás (in-doolahsh)

The airplane   A repülőgép, a gép (o reppewlu[r]
                                        gehp, o gehp)
I want to confirm a reservation on   Szeretnék érvenyesíteni egy
   flight number . . . for . . .   rezervációt a . . . járatszámon
                                        . . . ba. (serretnehk
                                        ehrven-yesheeteni edge
                                        rezervahtsioht o . . .
                                        yahrot-sahmohn . . . bo.)
Where is the check-in?   A jegykezelés hol van? (o
                                        yedge-kezelehsh hohl von?)
I am checking in for . . .   Megyek . . . ba (medge-ek . . . bo.)
Fasten your seat-belt   Kösse össze a biztonsági ővét
                                        (ku[r]sheh u[r]sse o
                                        biztohnshahgi u[r]veht)

The railroad   A vasút (o voshoot)
From what track does the train to   Melyik vágányról indul a . . . -i
   . . . leave?   vonat? (meyik vahgahn-rohl
                                        indool o . . . -i vohnot?)
Which way is the dining-car?   Merre van az étkező-kocsi?
                                        (mehr-re von oz
                                        ehtkezu[r]-kohchi?)

Bus, streetcar, subway   Autóbusz, villamos, metró
                                        (owtohbooss, villamohsh,
                                        metro)
Does this bus go to . . . ?   Megy ez az autóbusz . . . felé?
                                        (medge ez oz owtobooss . . .
                                        feleh?)
Trolleybus   Trolibusz (trohlibooss)
I want to get off at . . . Street   Szeretnék leszállni . . . utcánál
                                        (seretnehk lehsahl-ni . . .
                                        ootsahnahl)
   at the next stop   a legközelebbi megállónál (o
                                        legku[r]zeleb-bi
                                        meg-ahl-lohnahl)

Taxi   Taxi (Toksi)
Please go to . . .   Kérem . . . -ba menni (Kehrem
                                        . . . -bo menni)
Stop at . . .   Álljon meg . . . -nál (Ahl-yon meg
                                        . . . -nahl)
Stop here   Álljon meg itt (Ahl-yon meg itt)

NUMBERS

1 egy (edge)
2 két, kettő (keht, *ket*-tu[r])
3 három (*hah*rohm)
4 négy (naydge)
5 öt (u[r]t)
11 tizenegy (*teez*enedge)
12 tizenkét, -kettő (*teez*enkeht, -*ket*-tu[r])
13 tizenhárom (*teez*enhahrom)
14 tizennégy (*teez*en-naydge)
15 tizenöt (*teez*enu[r]t)
16 tizenhat (*teez*enhot)
17 tizenhét (*teez*enhayt)
18 tizennyolc (*teez*en-nyolts)
19 tizenkilenc (*teez*en-kilents)
20 húsz (hooss)
25 huszonöt (*hoos*sohnu[r]t)
30 harminc (*horr*-mints)
40 negyven (*nedge*-ven)
50 ötven (u[r]t-ven)

6 hat (hot)
7 hét (hayt)
8 nyolc (nyohlts)
9 kilenc (*kil*ents)
10 tíz (teez)
60 hatvan (*hot*-von)
70 hetven (*het*-ven)
80 nyolcvan (*nyohlts*-von)
90 kilencven (*kil*ents-ven)
100 száz (sahz)
200 kétszáz (*keht*-sahz)
300 háromszáz (*hah*rohm-sahz)
400 négyszáz (*naydge*-sahz)
500 ötszáz (u[r]t-sahz)
600 hatszáz (*hot*-sahz)
700 hétszáz (*heht*-sahz)
800 nyolcszáz (*nyohlts*-sahz)
900 kilencszáz (*kil*ents-sahz)
1,000 ezer (*ezehr*)

DAYS OF THE WEEK

Sunday — vasárnap (*vosh*ahrnop)
Monday — hétfő (*heht*-fu(r))
Tuesday — kedd (ked)
Wednesday — szerda (*sehr*-do)
Thursday — csütörtok (*chew*-turtu (r)k)
Friday — péntek (pehn-tek)
Saturday — szombat (*sohm*-bot)

Index

INDEX

General and Practical Information

Geographic and Practical Information

ATLAS

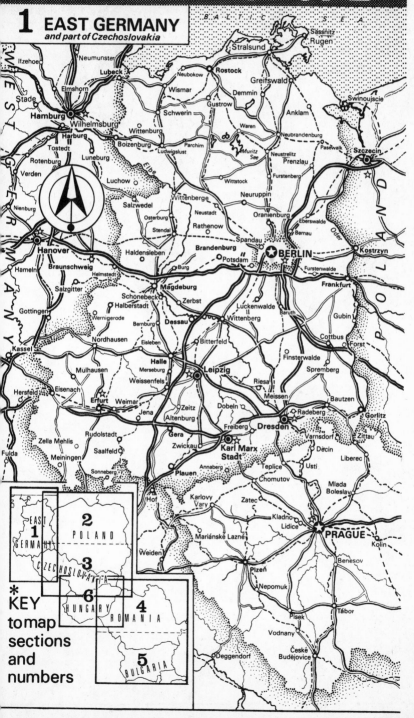

EASTERN EUROPE

1 EAST GERMANY
and part of Czechoslovakia

BALTIC SEA

*KEY to map sections and numbers

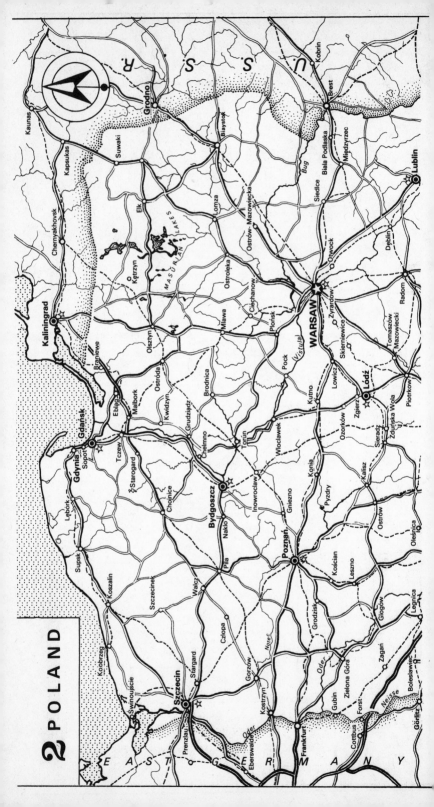

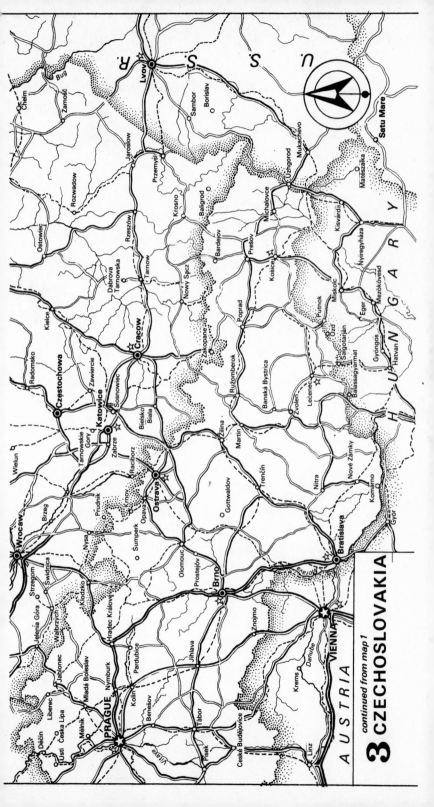

continued from map 1

3 CZECHOSLOVAKIA

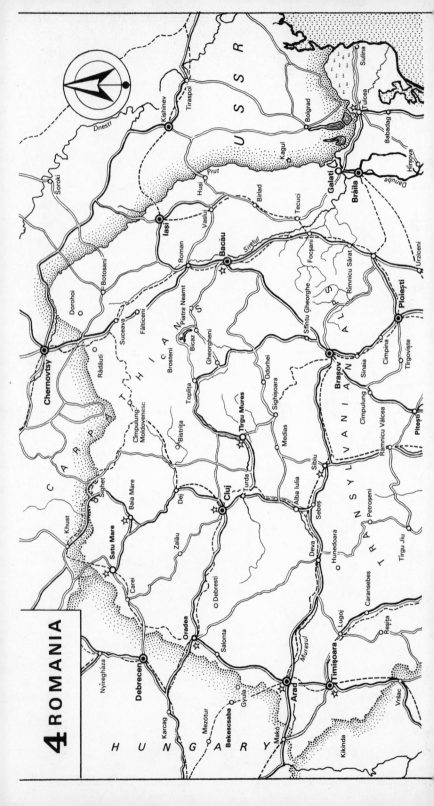

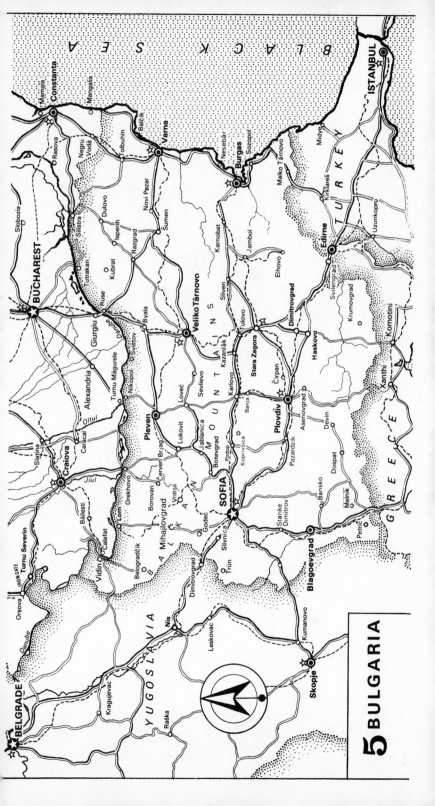

5 BULGARIA

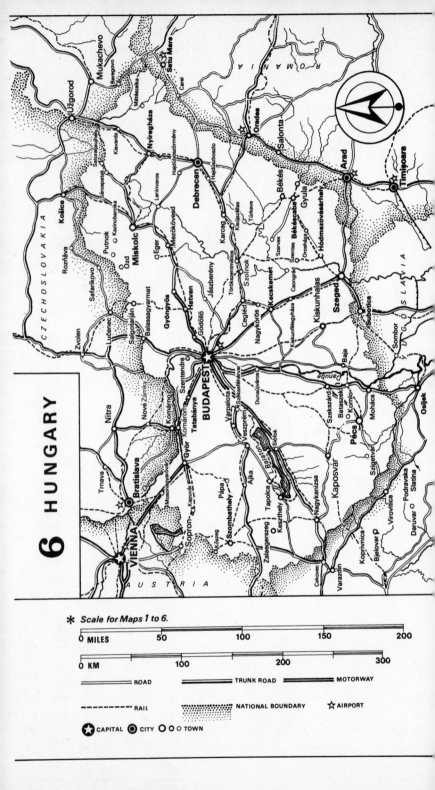

6 HUNGARY

ROMANIA

CZECHOSLOVAKIA

AUSTRIA

YUGOSLAVIA

Mukachevo
Satu Mare
Užgorod
Beregovo
Nyíregyháza
Cehel
Kisvárda
Sátoraljaújhely
Mátészalka
Oradea
Salonta
Hajdúszoboszló
Hajdúnánás
Arad
Timişoara
Košice
Putnok
Kazincbarcika
Miskolc
Debrecen
Kisújszállás
Túrkeve
Békés
Gyula
Rožňava
Ózd
Eger
Mezőkövesd
Karcag
Szarvas
Hódmezővásárhely
Šafárikovo
Zvolen
Lučenec
Salgótarján
Balassagyarmat
Gyöngyös
Hatvan
Jászberény
Szolnok
Törökszentmiklós
Mezőtúr
Csongrád
Orosháza
Békéscsaba
Szentes
Subotica
Szeged
Kiskunfélegyháza
Sombor
Zólyom
Nitra
Nové Zámky
Komárno
Komárom
Esztergom
Szentendre
Vác
Gödöllő
Cegléd
Nagykőrös
Kecskemét
Kiskunhalas
Baja
Trnava
Bratislava
Dunaújváros
Szekszárd
Bátaszék
Komló
Mohács
Pécs
VIENNA
Mosonmagyaróvár
Győr
Kapuvár
Pápa
Tatabánya
Várpalota
Székesfehérvár
Veszprém
Siófok
Kaposvár
Szigetvár
Osijek
Sopron
Szombathely
Ajka
Tapolca
Keszthely
Nagykanizsa
Podravska
Kőszeg
Zalaegerszeg
L. Balaton
Varaždin
Koprivnica
Virovitica
Daruvar
Slatina
Čakovec
Bjelovar
BUDAPEST
Danube
Dráva

* Scale for Maps 1 to 6.

0 MILES 50 100 150 200

0 KM 100 200 300

—————— ROAD ══════ TRUNK ROAD ═══════ MOTORWAY

------ RAIL ········· NATIONAL BOUNDARY ☆ AIRPORT

⊛ CAPITAL ◉ CITY ○○○ TOWN

Fodor's Travel Guides

U.S. Guides

Alaska
American Cities
The American South
Arizona
Atlantic City & the
  New Jersey Shore
Boston
California
Cape Cod
Carolinas & the
  Georgia Coast
Chesapeake
Chicago
Colorado
Dallas & Fort Worth
Disney World & the
  Orlando Area

The Far West
Florida
Greater Miami,
  Fort Lauderdale,
  Palm Beach
Hawaii
Hawaii (Great Travel
  Values)
Houston & Galveston
I-10: California to
  Florida
I-55: Chicago to New
  Orleans
I-75: Michigan to
  Florida
I-80: San Francisco to
  New York

I-95: Maine to Miami
Las Vegas
Los Angeles, Orange
  County, Palm Springs
Maui
New England
New Mexico
New Orleans
New Orleans (Pocket
  Guide)
New York City
New York City (Pocket
  Guide)
New York State
Pacific North Coast
Philadelphia
Puerto Rico (Fun in)

Rockies
San Diego
San Francisco
San Francisco (Pocket
  Guide)
Texas
United States of
  America
Virgin Islands
  (U.S. & British)
Virginia
Waikiki
Washington, DC
Williamsburg,
  Jamestown &
  Yorktown

Foreign Guides

Acapulco
Amsterdam
Australia, New Zealand
  & the South Pacific
Austria
The Bahamas
The Bahamas (Pocket
  Guide)
Barbados (Fun in)
Beijing, Guangzhou &
  Shanghai
Belgium & Luxembourg
Bermuda
Brazil
Britain (Great Travel
  Values)
Canada
Canada (Great Travel
  Values)
Canada's Maritime
  Provinces
Cancún, Cozumel,
  Mérida, The
  Yucatán
Caribbean
Caribbean (Great
  Travel Values)

Central America
Copenhagen,
  Stockholm, Oslo,
  Helsinki, Reykjavik
Eastern Europe
Egypt
Europe
Europe (Budget)
Florence & Venice
France
France (Great Travel
  Values)
Germany
Germany (Great Travel
  Values)
Great Britain
Greece
Holland
Hong Kong & Macau
Hungary
India
Ireland
Israel
Italy
Italy (Great Travel
  Values)
Jamaica (Fun in)

Japan
Japan (Great Travel
  Values)
Jordan & the Holy Land
Kenya
Korea
Lisbon
Loire Valley
London
London (Pocket Guide)
London (Great Travel
  Values)
Madrid
Mexico
Mexico (Great Travel
  Values)
Mexico City & Acapulco
Mexico's Baja & Puerto
  Vallarta, Mazatlán,
  Manzanillo, Copper
  Canyon
Montreal
Munich
New Zealand
North Africa
Paris
Paris (Pocket Guide)

People's Republic of
  China
Portugal
Province of Quebec
Rio de Janeiro
The Riviera (Fun on)
Rome
St. Martin/St. Maarten
Scandinavia
Scotland
Singapore
South America
South Pacific
Southeast Asia
Soviet Union
Spain
Spain (Great Travel
  Values)
Sweden
Switzerland
Sydney
Tokyo
Toronto
Turkey
Vienna
Yugoslavia

Special-Interest Guides

Bed & Breakfast
  Guide: North America
1936...On the
  Continent

Royalty Watching
Selected Hotels of
  Europe

Selected Resorts
  and Hotels of the U.S.
Ski Resorts of North
  America

Views to Dine by
  around the World